Using Microsoft Publisher

2023 Edition

Kevin Wilson

Elluminet Press
www.elluminetpress.com

Using Microsoft Publisher: 2023 Ed

Publisher: Elluminet Press
Director: Kevin Wilson
Lead Editor: Steven Ashmore
Technical Reviewer: Mike Taylor, Robert Ashcroft
Copy Editors: Joanne Taylor, James Marsh
Proof Reader: Mike Taylor
Indexer: James Marsh
Cover Designer: Kevin Wilson

eBook versions and licenses are also available for most titles. Any source code or other supplementary materials referenced by the author in this text is available to readers at

www.elluminetpress.com/resources

For detailed information about how to locate your book's source code, go to

www.elluminetpress.com/resources

Table of Contents

About the Author

With over 20 years' experience in the computer industry, Kevin Wilson has made a career out of technology and showing others how to use it. After earning a master's degree in computer science, software engineering, and multimedia systems, Kevin has held various positions in the IT industry including graphic & web design, digital film & photography, programming & software engineering, developing & managing corporate networks, building computer systems, and IT support.

He serves as senior writer and director at Elluminet Press Ltd, he periodically teaches computer science at college, and works as an IT trainer in England while researching for his PhD. His books have become a valuable resource among the students in England, South Africa, Canada, and in the United States.

Kevin's motto is clear: "If you can't explain something simply, then you haven't understood it well enough." To that end, he has created the Exploring Tech Computing series, in which he breaks down complex technological subjects into smaller, easy-to-follow steps that students and ordinary computer users can put into practice.

Acknowledgements

Thanks to all the staff at Luminescent Media & Elluminet Press for their passion, dedication and hard work in the preparation and production of this book.

To all my friends and family for their continued support and encouragement in all my writing projects.

To all my colleagues, students and testers who took the time to test procedures and offer feedback on the book

Finally thanks to you the reader for choosing this book. I hope it helps you to use your computer with greater understanding.

1 Microsoft Publisher

Microsoft Publisher is a desktop publishing application developed by Microsoft. It is considered an entry level desktop publishing application and is aimed at home users, schools, and small businesses for creating a wide range of printed and digital materials, such as brochures, flyers, newsletters, posters, greeting cards, and business stationery. Many of these are included with Publisher as a template that you can edit and customise. You can also create your own design from scratch.

Unlike other Office applications such as Word, Publisher focuses more on page layout and design, rather than text composition and proofing.

It's also worth noting that Microsoft Publisher is only available for Windows, and is not included in versions of Microsoft Office for other operating systems.

Publisher offers various features and tools to create and edit publications. These tools are all grouped into tabs in a menu system along the top of the screen called a ribbon.

Utilizing a WYSIWYG (What-You-See-Is-What-You-Get) interface, Publisher ensures that what you design on the screen will closely resemble the final printed output. This feature allows for accurate representation during the creative process.

With Publisher, you have the freedom to arrange your designs on the page using various objects such as text boxes for headings and body text, image place-holders for photographs, and shapes for added visual elements. Additionally, Publisher offers a selection of pre-designed templates and building blocks known as "page parts" for streamlining the creation of more extensive publications.

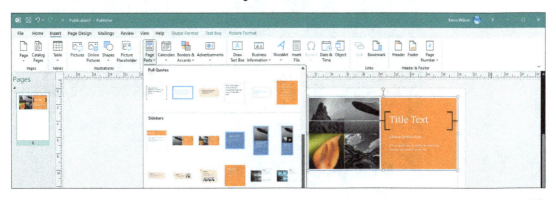

To maintain the quality of your work, there are proofing tools such as spelling and grammar checks. These tools highlight potentially misspelled words with red underlines and mark grammar errors with green indicators. Auto-correct features are also available to rectify common misspellings or phrases, enhancing the overall accuracy and professionalism of your publications.

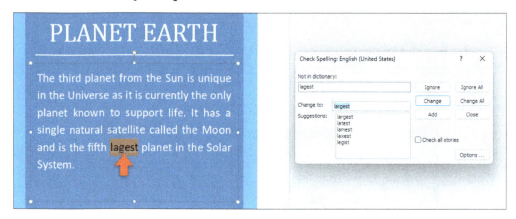

You can use advanced typography beyond what's typically available in word processors. This includes kerning, which is the space between specific pairs of characters, and tracking, which adjusts spacing uniformly over a range of characters. As well as the ability to use OpenType fonts and features such as stylistic sets, ligatures, and drop caps, which are crucial for professional-looking text layout.

In educational settings, Publisher serves as a practical tool for students and teachers to create materials for their lessons. Its ease of use makes it suitable for classroom settings where the primary focus is on content rather than learning complex software. While Microsoft Publisher is suitable for small businesses, education and individual users, it is not as feature-rich or versatile as professional desktop publishing (DTP) software such as Adobe InDesign, however Publisher is ideal for basic to intermediate desktop publishing tasks.

Publisher allows you to convert your projects into various file formats suitable for different purposes:

PDF is one of the most common methods for sharing Publisher documents. PDFs can be opened on almost any device with free software, and they preserve the layout, fonts, and images of your document as they were designed.

Image Formats (JPG, PNG, TIFF): Publisher allows you to export pages as images. This is useful when you need to include a page from your publication in a web page or share it as a picture on social media.

Pack and Go prepares your Publisher file and associated resources for a commercial printer. It can include all the necessary fonts and linked graphics to ensure that the document prints correctly.

The export option you use depends on whether it's for digital viewing (PDF/image), print production (PDF), commercial printing (pack and go/PDF), or for the web (image).

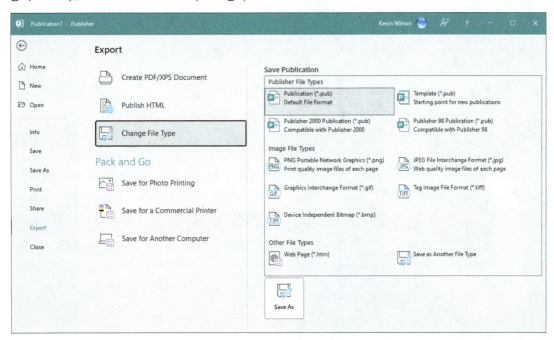

2

Getting around Publisher

Microsoft Publisher is a desktop publishing application developed by Microsoft. Publisher is considered an entry level desktop publishing application and is aimed at home users, schools, and small businesses with in house printing. Publisher is not used for commercial printing purposes.

In this chapter, we'll take a look at

- Starting Publisher

- Create a Shortcut

- Home Screen

- New Sidebar

- Open Sidebar

- Main Screen

- The Ribbon Menu

- File Backstage

Have a look at the video resources. Open your web browser and navigate to the following website.

elluminetpress.com/start-pub

Starting Publisher

Once you have Microsoft Office installed, you'll find Publisher on your start menu.

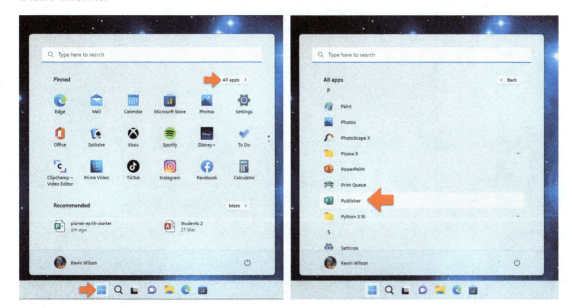

Create a Shortcut

To make things easier, you can pin the Publisher icon to your task bar. I find this feature useful. To do this, with Publisher running, right click on the Publisher icon on the taskbar then click 'pin to taskbar'.

This way, Publisher is always on the taskbar whenever you need it.

Home Screen

Once Publisher opens, you'll land on the home screen. Here you can open a blank publication or select a template. Underneath, you'll see a list of all your recently opened publications.

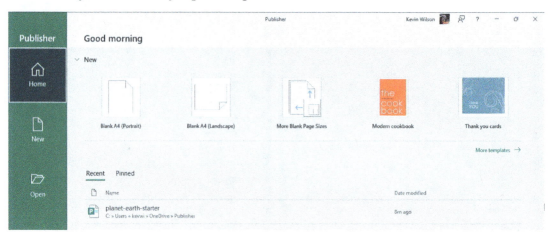

You can also pin publications to the 'pinned' list. The pinned list is used to list publications you use all the time for quick access. To pin a publication, right click on the file in the 'recent' list then select 'pin to list'.

New Sidebar

To create a new publication or use a template, select 'new' from the panel on the left hand side.

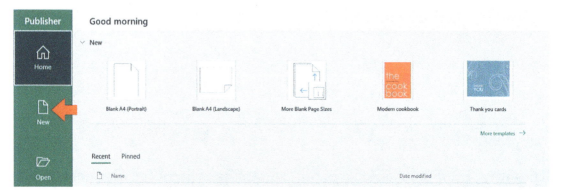

Along the top, you can create a new blank publication in portrait or landscape orientation using the default page size, or you can create a blank publication using another page size.

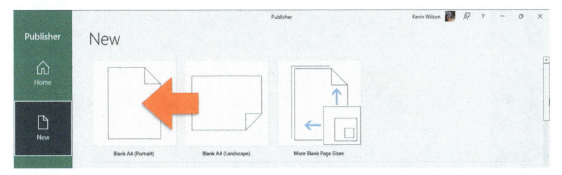

Underneath, you can select a template.

Use the search field to search for a particular template.

Here, I'm searching for a party invite.

To create a blank publication, select 'blank' from the options along the top of the screen.

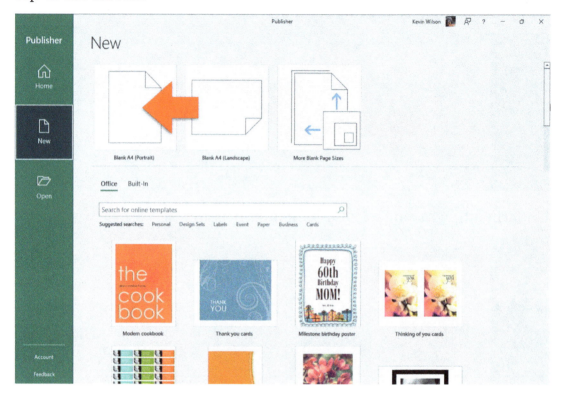

Open Sidebar

To open any saved publications, select 'open' from the sidebar on the left hand side.

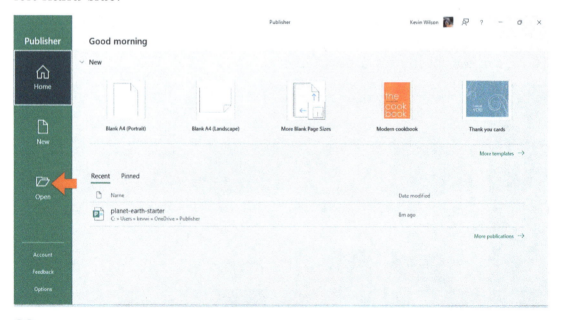

On the left panel you'll see some options as to where you can open a publication from. You can open a publication from the recently used file list...

...or publications saved on your OneDrive.

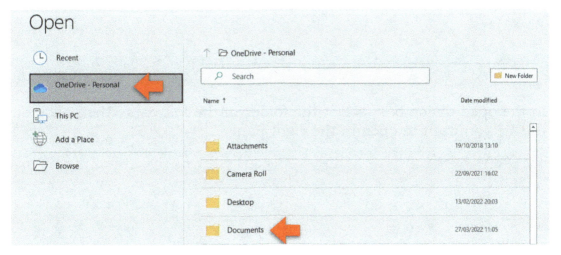

Or publications saved on your PC. Select 'this pc', then browse through the files on the right.

You can also browse for files anywhere on your PC. To do this, click 'browse'.

In the open dialog box, select the folder in the left pane, then click on the file you want to open in the right pane.

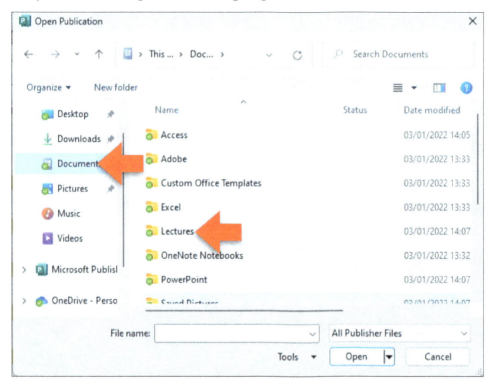

Click 'open'.

Main Screen

Lets take a look at Publisher's main screen. Here we can see, illustrated below, the screen is divided into sections.

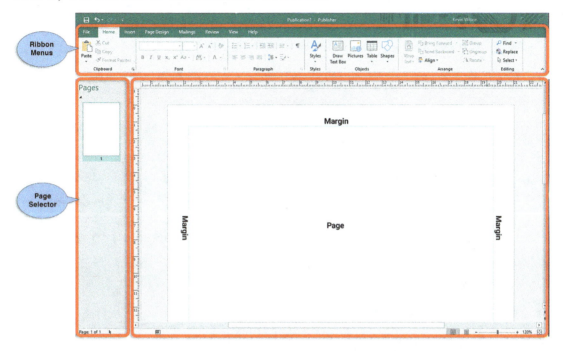

The page selector down the left hand side, shows all pages you've created in your publication. You can also use this panel to select the pages you want to view or edit.

In the main area on the right, you'll see your page. This is where you create your publication.

On the bottom left of the screen you'll see three sets of values. The first shows you the page number you're on, the second set shows you the position of the top left corner of an object you've selected.

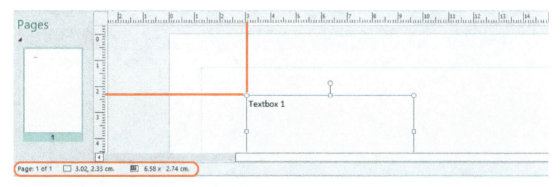

The second set of numbers shows the size of the selected object.

On the bottom right, you'll see some controls that allow you to view your publication as a single page, or as a two page spread - useful if you're working with booklets.

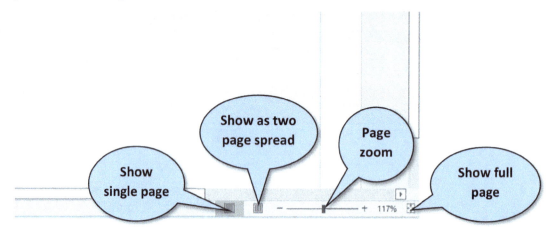

Next to that, you'll see the zoom controls. This allows you to zoom into your page.

The Ribbon Menu

Your tools are grouped into tabs called ribbons along the top of the screen. Tools are grouped according to their function.

Home Ribbon Tab

All tools to do with text formatting, for example, making text bold, changing fonts, and the most common tools for text alignment, and formatting.

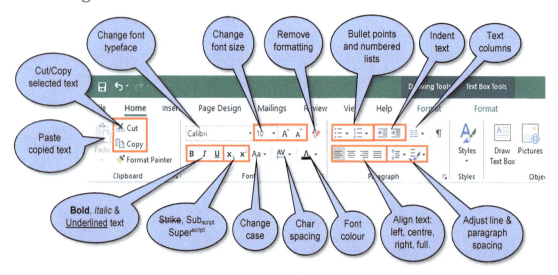

Insert Ribbon Tab

All tools to do with inserting photos, graphics, tables, charts, and borders etc.

You can also insert equations, word art, pre-designed ads, graphic 'page parts', and smart art using the 'illustrations' and 'building blocks' section of the ribbon.

 and

You can add text boxes, symbols, and word art using the 'text' section of the ribbon.

Page Design Ribbon Tab

The page design ribbon allows you to change templates, adjust margins, page orientation, size, and set up design guides to help you align the elements on your page.

You can also select pre-designed colour schemes, change the background and set up page masters.

Mailings Ribbon

The mailings ribbon allows you to create mail merges in your publisher document and link it to a data source in a spreadsheet or database.

Review Ribbon Tab

With the review ribbon, you can spell check your document, look up words in the thesaurus, translate text into another language, or do some research.

View Ribbon Tab

With the view ribbon you can change your default view, open master pages, add rulers, navigation, and zoom.

Shape Format Ribbon Tab

The shape format ribbon tab appears when you select a shape such as a circle, rectangle or text box you've inserted into your publication. This is where you can change the shape itself, shape fill color, outline color and an effect such as a shadow.

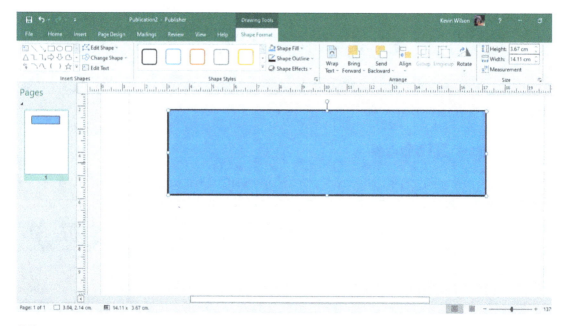

Picture Format Ribbon Tab

The picture format ribbon tab appears when you select a photo or image you've inserted into a publication. This is where you can style the photo or image you've inserted.

You can add a border, recolor the picture, change the brightness, or contract, add a caption and wrap text.

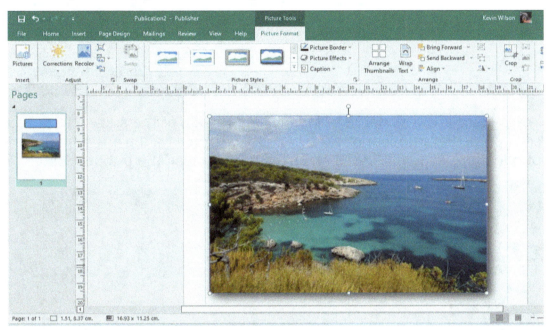

Text Box Ribbon Tab

The text box ribbon tab appears when you select a text box you've inserted into a publication. Here, you can change the font, text color, highlight, text box background color and border color, as well as the text box margins and alignment.

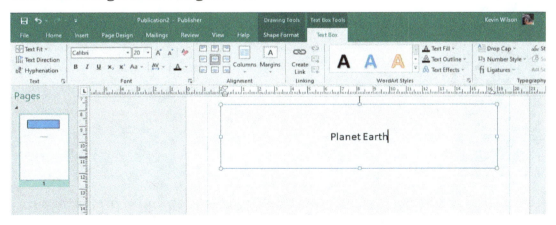

File Backstage

If you click 'File' on the top left of your screen, this will open up what Microsoft call the backstage.

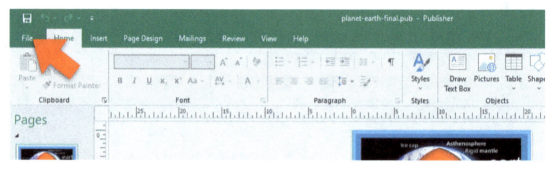

You'll see a green panel down the left hand side of the stage. Here, you can open a new publication. You can also get information on your current publication, as well as save, print, share, or close the publication.

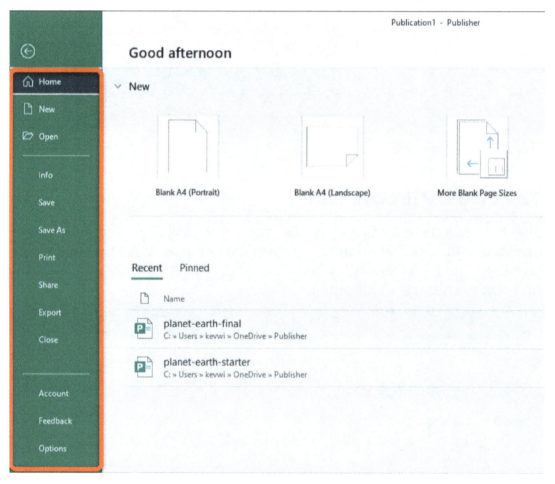

You can also access your account settings and options/preferences.

Info

Selecting info from the panel on the left will display statistics and other information about the publication you have open.

Save and Save As

Selecting save from the panel on the left will save the publication using the same filename. Save as will save the publication as a new file with a different file name.

Print

Selecting print from the panel on the left will print your publication out to your printer or to PDF

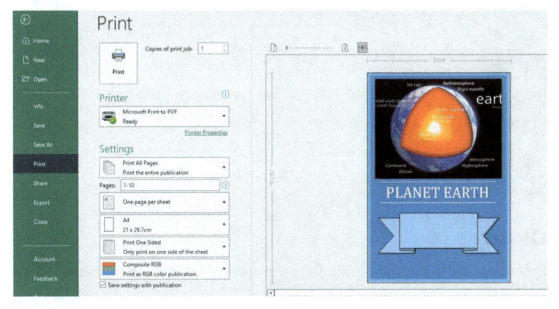

Share

Selecting share from the panel on the left will allow you to share your publication with someone else using email

Export

Selecting export from the panel on the left will allow you to export your publication as a different file format such as PDF, HTML or commercial printing

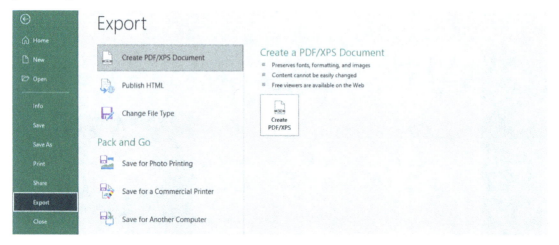

Close

Selecting close from the panel on the left will close the currently open publication.

Options

Selecting options will show system preferences and customisations you can apply to publisher.

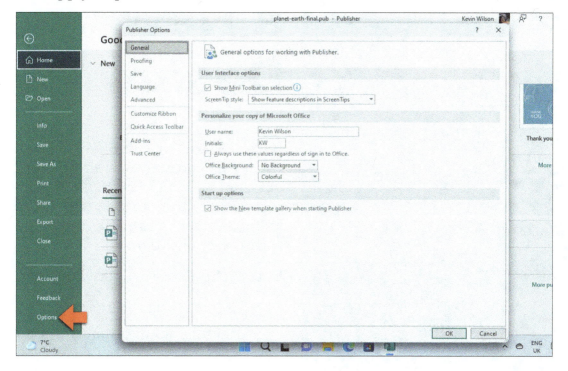

Account

Selecting account will allow you to sign into or out of your Microsoft Account, register Office, update and activate Office.

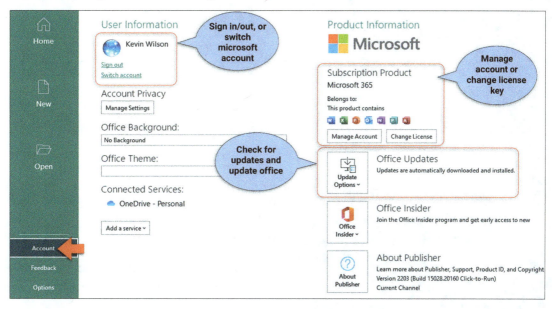

3

Building a New Design

With Microsoft Publisher, you can easily create various different designs. You can design them from scratch, or you can use one of the many different templates included with the application.

In this chapter, we'll take a look at

- Basic Design Principles
- Adding and formatting Text Box
- Typography Features
- Text Effects
- Formatting Text Boxes
- Manipulating Text Boxes
- Tables
- Border Art
- Layout Guides

Check out the video resources. Open your browser and navigate to:

elluminetpress.com/building-pub

For this section you'll need the files from:

elluminetpress.com/ms-pub

Scroll down to the file resources section and download the files.

Basic Design Principles

Before we start building publications, lets start by having a look at some basic design principals. This will help you create visually appealing and effective publications in Microsoft Publisher. Understanding these principles is key to enhancing the impact of your work. Remember, effective design is all about clear communication, visual appeal, and creating an enjoyable experience for your audience. The first four points below are known as the CRAP principles of graphic design.

Contrast

Contrast involves making elements stand out by using opposite or complementary elements and colors.

Use light colors on dark backgrounds or vice versa. Combine different sizes of elements to draw attention. Vary font types and weights. Be careful not to use clashing colors such as red and green or red and blue.

Repetition

Repetition involves repeating visual elements of the design throughout the publication. This creates a sense of unity and consistency, reinforcing brand identity or the publication's theme.

As you can see in the example below, we've repeat design elements such color schemes, fonts, and graphic elements to create a visually cohesive document. Here, we've used consistent font sizes and styles. The photos are of a similar style and feature the same people. The text boxes have a consistent blue background with white text.

TRADER NEWS

A monthly newsletter brought to you by Elluminet Press Ltd

THE NEWS

Lorem ipsum dolor sit amet, consectetur adipisicing elit, sed do eiusmod tempor incididunt ut labore et dolore magna aliqua. Ut enim ad minim veniam, quis nostrud exercitation ullamco laboris nisi ut aliquip ex ea commodo consequat. Duis aute irure dolor in reprehenderit in voluptate velit esse cillum dolore eu fugiat nulla pariatur.

Excepteur sint occaecat cupidatat non proident, sunt in culpa qui officia deserunt mollit anim id est laborum. Sed ut perspiciatis unde omnis iste natus error sit voluptatem accusantium doloremque laudantium, totam rem aperiam, eaque ipsa quae ab illo inventore veritatis et quasi architecto beatae vitae dicta sunt explicabo. Nemo enim ipsam voluptatem quia voluptas sit aspernatur aut odit aut fugit, sed quia consequuntur magni dolores eos qui ratione voluptatem sequi nesciunt. Neque porro quisquam est, qui dolorem ipsum quia dolor

OUR GOALS THIS WEEK

Lorem ipsum dolor sit amet, consectetur adipisicing elit, sed do eiusmod tempor incididunt ut labore et dolore magna aliqua. Ut enim ad minim veniam, quis nostrud exercitation ullamco laboris nisi ut aliquip ex ea commodo consequat. Duis aute irure dolor in reprehenderit in voluptate velit esse cillum dolore eu fugiat nulla pariatur.

Excepteur sint occaecat cupidatat non proident, sunt in culpa qui officia deserunt mollit anim id est

Alignment

Alignment arranges elements in a sharp, orderly manner, aligning them with a top, bottom, center, or side edge. Edge Alignment aligns elements along a common edge. Center Alignment aligns elements around a central line.

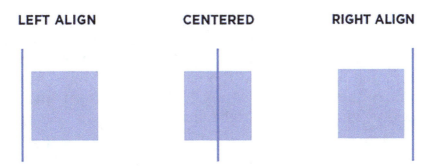

Consistent alignment creates a cohesive, organized look. Align text blocks with images or other page elements to achieve visual harmony. Here in our newsletter below, we can see that the left and right edges are all aligned. You'll also notice that the sub heading 'a monthly newsletter brought to you by Elluminet Press Ltd' is aligned to the center in the blue rectangle.

The image in the middle is aligned with the text box. The text is aligned with the left and right margins of the textbox (fully justified)

Proximity

Proximity groups related items together, creating a connection between them. This helps organize information, reduces clutter, and increases the viewer's understanding. Group related elements, like captions with images or related points in a list, to create clear, logical sections.

In the flyer below, information is grouped and organised the information. The main theme "Campus Band Battle" is in the largest text as it's the main eye catcher used to inform people what the flyer is about. Vital information such as the date of the event and the venue are grouped together under the title in bold text. Other important information is grouped in the side bar on the right hand side.

In order to distinguish the different information that this flyer is communicating, we've used color and white space to group the information logically.

White space, or negative space, is the unmarked space between elements. The use of white space is crucial in giving a design a polished look. Effective use of space can help to highlight important elements and make a design more legible and easier to take in.

Balance

Balance refers to the distribution of visual elements, ensuring that no part of the design overwhelms others. It's about creating a sense of equilibrium. Use balance to guide the reader's focus.

Symmetrical balance mirrors elements on either side of an axis. It conveys formality and stability.

Asymmetrical balance involves different elements that have equal visual weight; it's more dynamic and interesting.

Heirarchy

Hierarchy is the arrangement of elements in a way that implies importance.

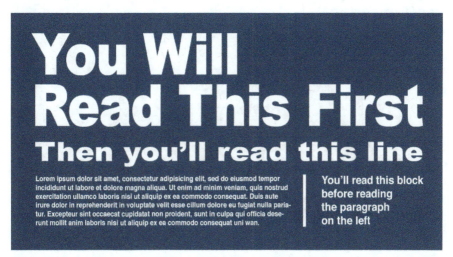

Use size, color, and placement to direct the viewer's attention. Make titles large and bold, subheadings smaller yet noticeable, and body text in a standard, readable size.

Proportion

Proportion refers to the relative size and scale of the various elements in a design. It's about the relationship between objects, or parts of objects, in terms of their size, quantity, or degree.

It is used to create a sense of unity, to manipulate how a design is perceived, and to help the audience prioritize different elements. For example, larger elements are often seen as more important than smaller ones.

Emphasis

Emphasis in design refers to creating a focal point and is about making a particular element stand out to draw the viewer's attention (such as the bold title in the slide below). It is typically used to highlight the most important part of a design, which could be a message, brand name, or key image. This principle ensures that the viewer's eye is drawn to what's most important.

Emphasis can be achieved through various means, such as using contrasting colors, larger or bolder fonts, or unique positioning. The use of negative space can also highlight an emphasized element.

Typography

Typography is the art of arranging letters and characters in a legible, readable and appealing way.

Publisher includes various typography features to help you format your text. It's important to note that these effects only work with certain fonts, such as Calibri, Cambria, Gabriola, Garamond, and Zapfino.

Typeface Anatomy

The x-height measures the height of lowercase letters, the cap height measures the height of uppercase letters, the ascender is a character stroke that extends above the x-height (eg on letter 'h'), and a descender is a character stroke that descends below the x-height (eg on letter 'g').

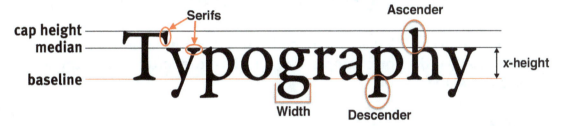

There are two types of font: Serif and Sans Serif. If you look at the sample above, you'll see on the letter 'T', there are little strokes or feet that finish off the ends of the letters. These are called serifs.

Garamond, Times New Roman, and Georgia are examples of serif fonts.

On the other hand a sans serif font doesn't have the strokes finishing off the end of the font.

Proxima Nova, Arial, and Helvetica are examples of sans serif fonts.

Chapter 3: Building a New Design

You'll find most designers will recommend using a sans serif font for headings, and a serif font for body text as serif fonts tend to be easier to read in a paragraph of text. However this isn't always the case. On many websites, the typeface used is sans serif giving a more modern look. In some newspapers you'll see serif fonts on headings and in the paragraphs of text.

Proportional vs Fixed

A proportional font contains characters that are of different widths. For example, the letter 'I' is much narrower than the letter 'O'. Most printed materials such as books use proportional fonts.

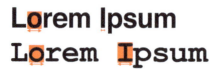

Fixed fonts, also called monospaced fonts contain characters that are of the same width. For example, the width of the letter 'I' and the letter 'O' are the same.

Leading

Leading (rhymes with 'heading') is the space between lines of text. This helps the eye move from the end of one line to the beginning of the next.

This is leading... Lorem ipsum dolor
sit amet, consectetur adipiscing elit,

Kerning & Tracking

Kerning is the process of adjusting the spacing between characters in a proportional font. For example:

Tr   Tr

Tracking is the uniform adjustment of the spacing of a word or block of text. For example:

T r a c k i n g   Tracking

Pitch

Pitch is the density of characters on a line and refers to the number of characters printed per inch.

Units of Measurement

You'll be familiar with inches and centimetres as units of measurement, but when working with printers and publishers you'll come across a few other units: points, picas, and pixels. Let's take a look at what these mean.

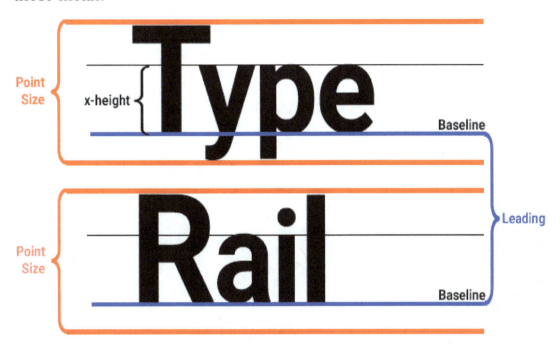

Points

A point is the smallest unit of measure in typesetting and is equal to 1/72 inch.

There are 72 points in 1 inch. Points are used for measuring font size, leading, and other items on a printed page.

Picas

A pica is equal to 12 points, or approximately 1⁄6 of an inch and is usually used for measuring lines of text.

Pixels

Pixel is short for picture element. Pixels are the little dots that make up an image on your screen.

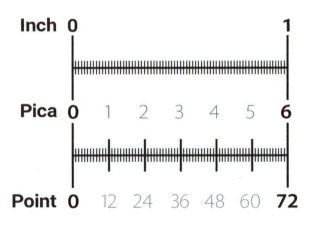

Creating a New Publication

Before you create a new publication you'll need to make a few decisions about certain aspects, such as page layout, paper type, and size.

Some of the first choices you need to make about your publication involve page layout. Creating a publication from a template takes care of most of these choices for you.

Size

Some publications, like flyers, can be small, A5 or A6. Other publications such as posters are a lot bigger, A3 or A1.

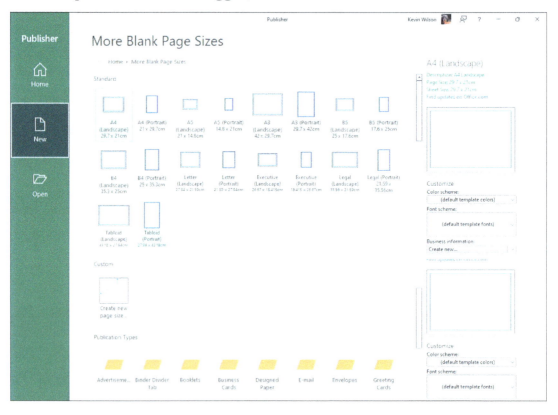

Orientation

Landscape or Portrait. Some flyers are portrait, as are most posters. Greetings cards can be both landscape and portrait orientation.

(Landscape)   (Portrait)

Margins

Margins are the areas of blank space around the top, bottom, left and right edges of a printed publication.

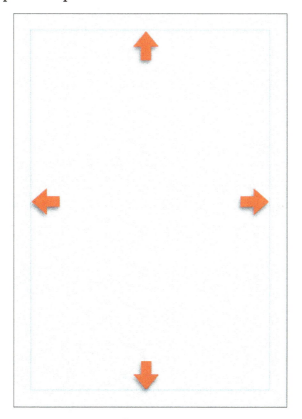

Open a New Publication

When you open publisher, you'll be able to select a template to start with or create a blank publication. Select 'new' from the panel on the left.

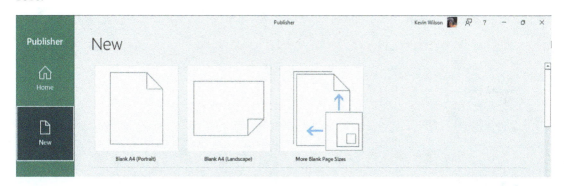

If you already have publisher running, click 'file' on the top left of the main screen, then select 'new'.

Click on a template. For this demo, we're going to use 'blank A4 (portrait)'.

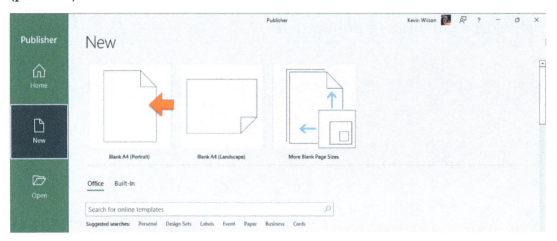

To select a different page size, click 'more blank page sizes', then select a size.

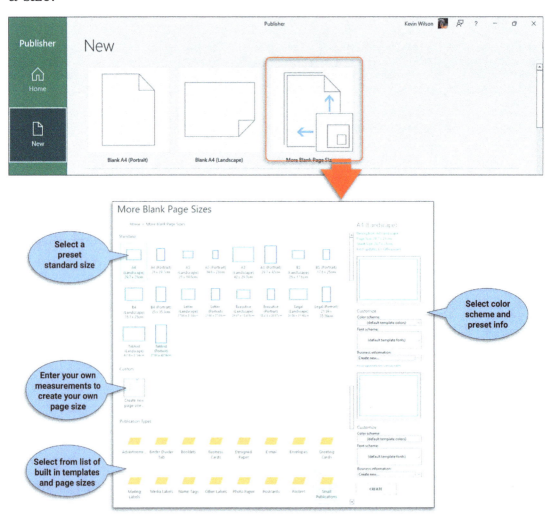

Once you've selected a template, you'll land on publisher's main work area.

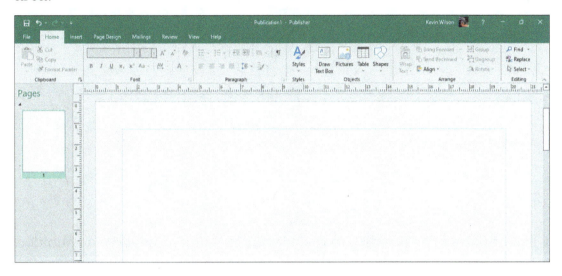

Here, we can start constructing our design. Let's take a look at some of the building blocks of a publication.

Basic Objects

Publisher documents are constructed using some basic elements. First is the text box. You can also add images, wordart, tables and shapes.

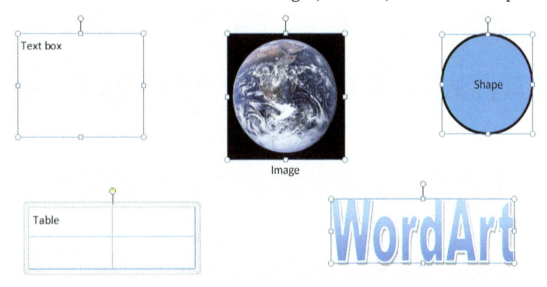

You can add text boxes to your design to contain the text and place it independently.

You can do the same with images and photos. These are used to place images within your design.

Chapter 3: Building a New Design

When you click on a text box, image or shape, a frame with small circles appear around the edge. These are called handles.

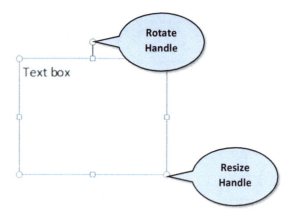

Click and drag the handles to resize your text box or image place holder.

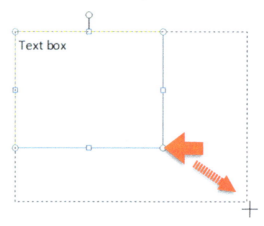

You can also rotate a shape. To do this, click and drag the rotate handle at the top of the shape.

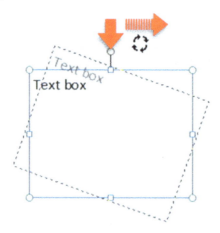

Now that we have explored the building blocks of a publication, lets create a design

Adding a Text Box

To add some text to your design, first you need to add a text box. To add a text box, go to the home ribbon and select 'draw text box'.

Click and drag to draw the text box on your page

Entering Text

Once you have inserted a text box, you can type in some text.

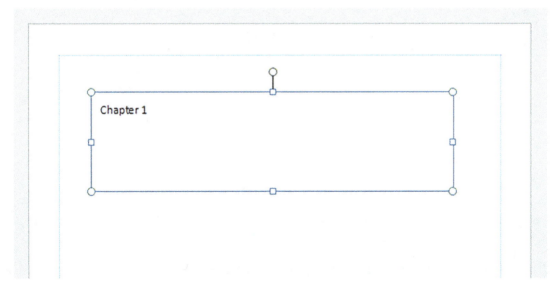

Formatting Text

Within your text box you can format your text. You can do this using the basic formatting tools on the home ribbon.

Changing Font

Highlight the text you want to change.

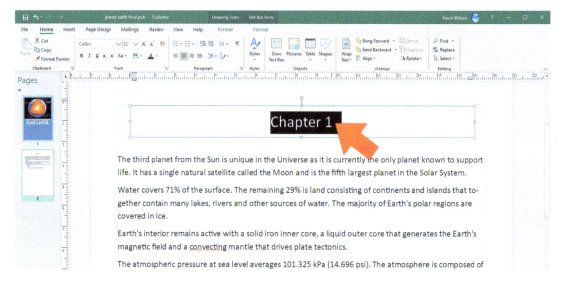

From the home ribbon click on the font name.

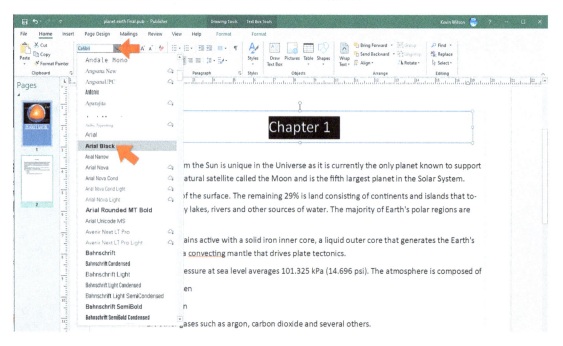

From the drop down box, select the font you want.

Font Size

Highlight the text you want to change.

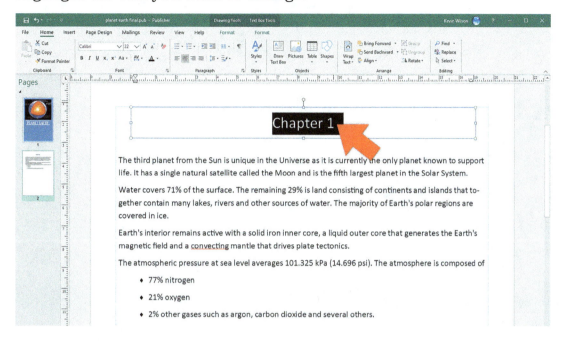

From the home ribbon, select the font size, then from the drop down select the size you want.

Bold, italic, underlined

Highlight the text you want to change.

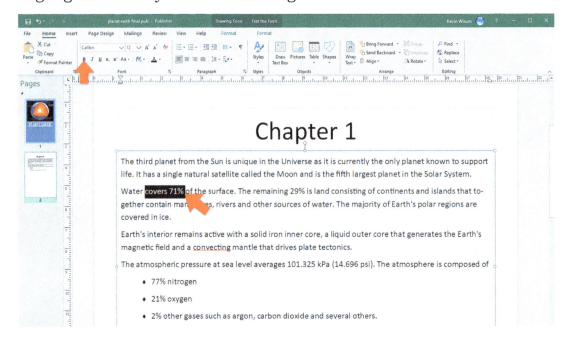

From the home ribbon, click the bold icon on the top left. Do the same for italic and underlined text.

Text Color

Highlight the text you want to change.

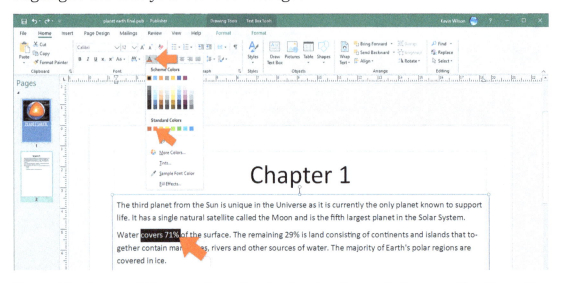

From the home ribbon, select the font color icon. Select a color from the drop down box.

Text Alignment

Within your text box you can align text to the left, middle, or the right. You can also fully justify text so a text block is aligned to both the left and right of the text box.

Water covers 71% of the surface. The remaining 29% is land consisting of continents and islands that together contain many lakes, rivers and other sources of water. The majority of Earth's polar regions are covered in ice.

Water covers 71% of the surface. The remaining 29% is land consisting of continents and islands that together contain many lakes, rivers and other sources of water. The majority of Earth's polar regions are covered in ice.

Water covers 71% of the surface. The remaining 29% is land consisting of continents and islands that together contain many lakes, rivers and other sources of water. The majority of Earth's polar regions are covered in ice.

Water covers 71% of the surface. The remaining 29% is land consisting of continents and islands that together contain many lakes, rivers and other sources of water. The majority of Earth's polar regions are covered in ice.

To do this, select the text you want to align.

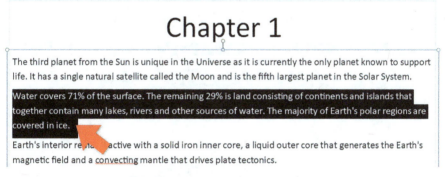

From the home ribbon, select a paragraph alignment icon.

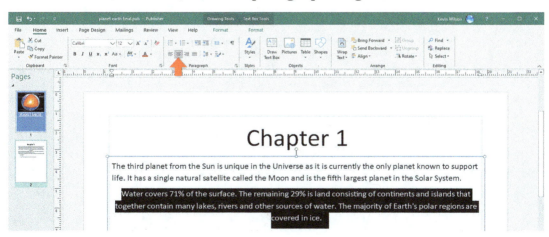

Change Case

You can quickly change the case of your text. You can change it to UPPERCASE, lowercase or Sentence case. To do this, select your text.

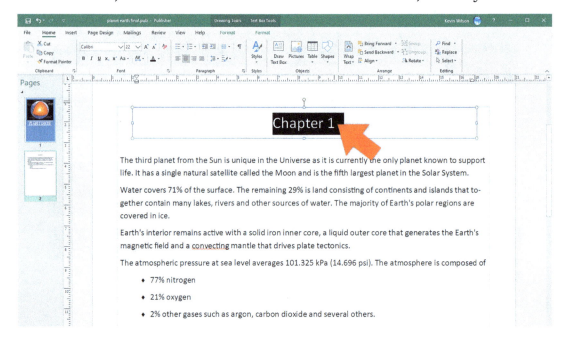

From the home ribbon, select the case change icon.

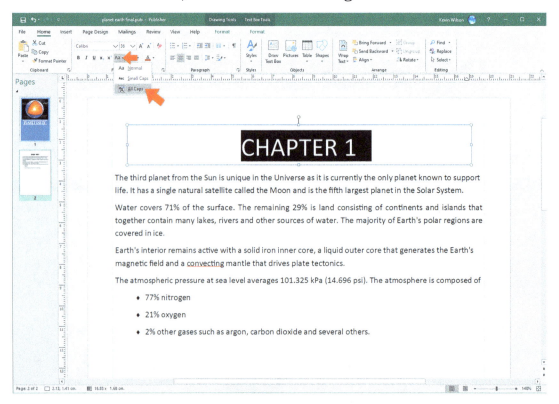

Drop Cap

A drop cap enlarges the first letter of the selected text and is often used at the start of a chapter or block of text. To do this, click on the paragraph you want to drop cap.

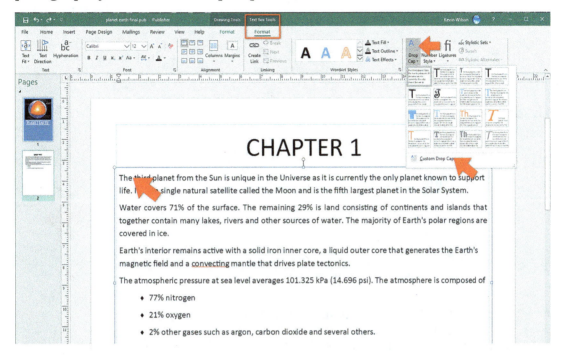

From the 'text box tools' format ribbon, select 'drop cap'. Now you can select a pre-set style from the options, or click 'custom drop cap'.

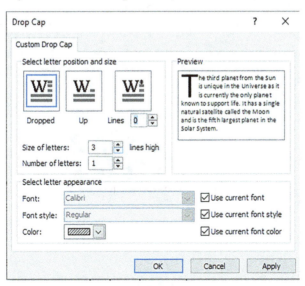

Change the size of letters to fit your drop cap into the paragraph, you can also change the font and color. Click 'apply' when you're done.

Stylistic Sets

These sets allow you choose between various styles for your fonts, usually in the form of exaggerated serifs or flourishes. Highlight the letter, then from the 'text box tools' format ribbon select 'stylistic sets'

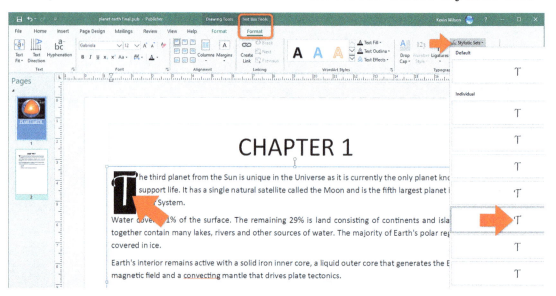

Select an option from the drop down box.

You can also use stylistic sets on words. Useful for creating fancy titles and headings.

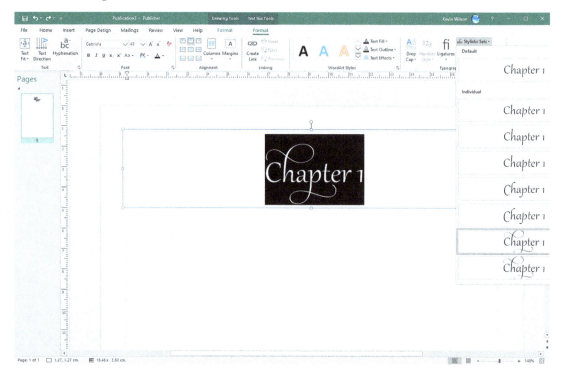

Ligatures

Ligatures connect certain combinations of letters to make them easier to read. There are many different ligatures: ct, ff, fi, ffi, st, sp, Th being the most common.

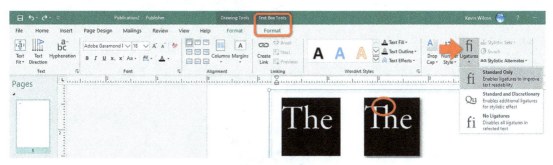

You can turn on ligatures from the 'text box tools' format ribbon. Select the character, then select 'ligatures'.

Stylistic Alternates

This offers different versions of specific letters. For example,

$$a \quad a$$
$$g \quad g$$

You'll find these alternatives on your 'text box tools' format ribbon. Select the character, then select 'stylistic Alternates'.

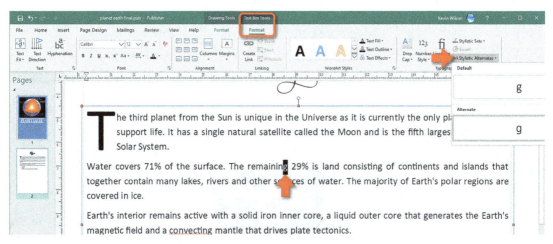

Text Effects

You can add drop shadows, reflections and bevels to your text, as well as change the style, add an outline and fill color.

Shadows

To add a shadow, select the text you want to use, then from the 'text box tools' format ribbon, select 'text effects'.

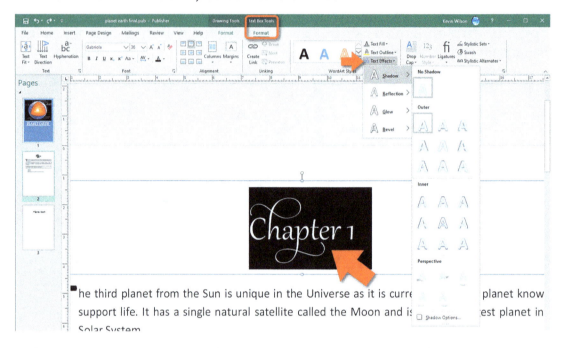

Select an effect from the list. You can also add a reflection, glow, or bevel effect from here.

Text Outline

To add a outline, select the text you want to use, then from the 'text box tools' format ribbon, select 'text outline'.

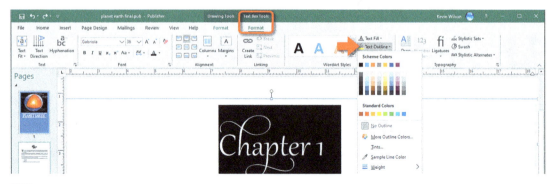

WordArt Styles

To use a wordart style, select the text you want to use, then from the 'text box tools' format ribbon, select a style from the wordart.

To view more styles, click the small down arrow next to the wordart styles.

You'll see the full list of options.

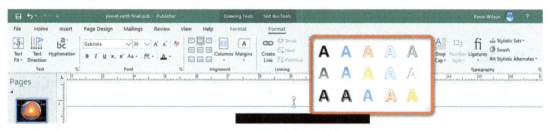

Select a style. You can select from a number of pre-defined styles.

third planet from the Sun is unique in the Universe as it is currently the only planet known to port life. It has a single natural satellite called the Moon and is the fifth largest planet in the

Formatting Text Boxes

You can add drop shadows, reflections and bevels to your text boxes, as well as change the style, add an outline and fill color.

Background Color

Select text box, then under 'drawing tools' select the 'format' ribbon. Select 'shape fill'.

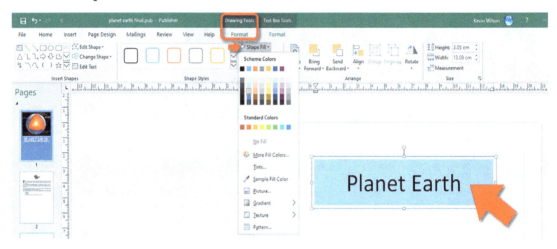

From the drop down menu, select a color.

Borders

Select text box, then under 'drawing tools' select the 'format' ribbon. Select 'shape outline'.

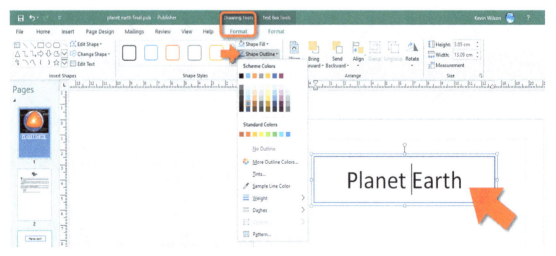

From the drop down menu, select a color.

Shadows

Select text box, then under 'drawing tools' select the 'format' ribbon. Select 'shape effects'.

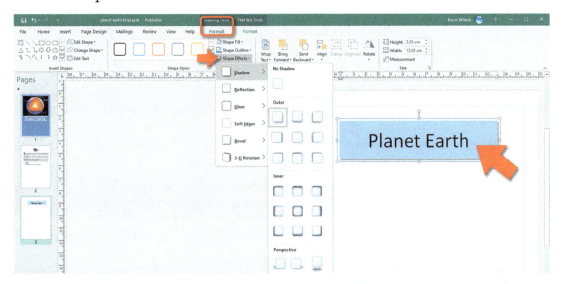

Go down to 'shadows', then select an effect from the slideout.

Styles

There are various pre-defined styles you can use to decorate your text boxes. To apply them, select text box, then under 'drawing tools' select the 'format' ribbon. Click the small arrow next to shape styles to open the panel.

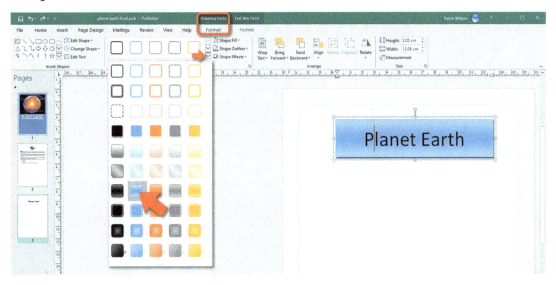

Select a style.

Textbox Margins

Each textbox has a margin at the top, bottom, left, and right hand side. This helps to pad out the text, especially if the textbox happens to have a border

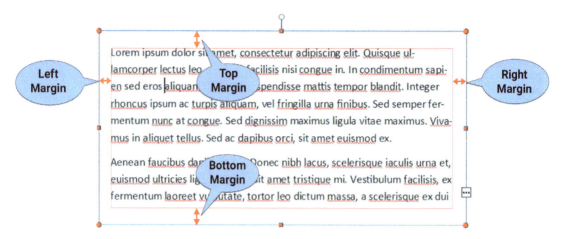

To adjust the borders, click on the text inside the textbox, then from the 'textbox' ribbon tab, select 'margins'.

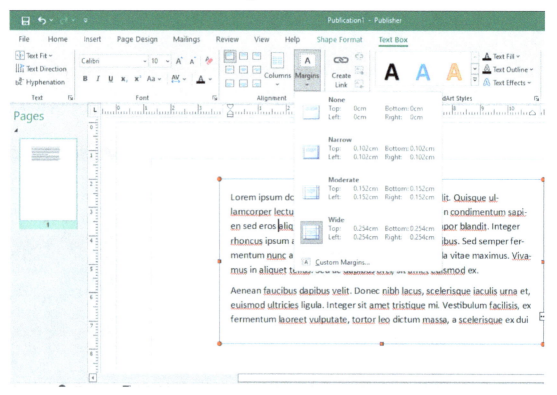

From the drop down menu, you can select preset margins, or if you want to enter your own measurements, select 'custom margins'.

From the 'textbox margins' section of the dialog box, enter the measurements for the margins. In the example below, I've adjusted the left hand margin to 1cm.

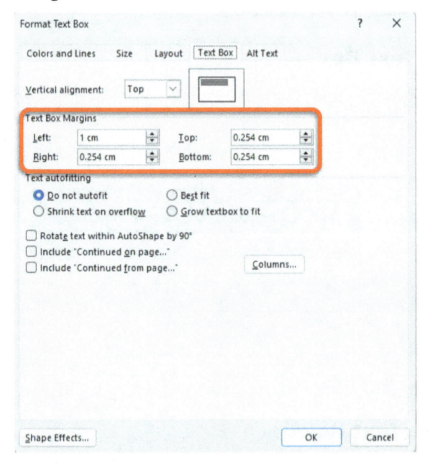

Here, you can see the left margin has moved

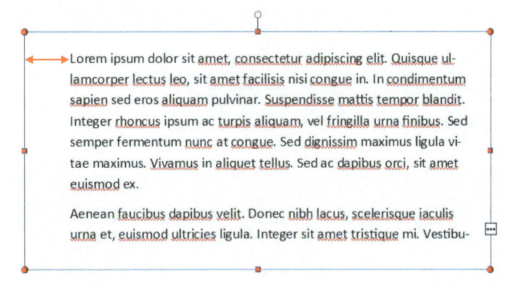

Manipulating Text Boxes

You can move, resize, and rotate text boxes, as well as change the text direction, margins and alignment.

Move Text Box

To move a text box, click on the text box's border. Drag the box to its new location.

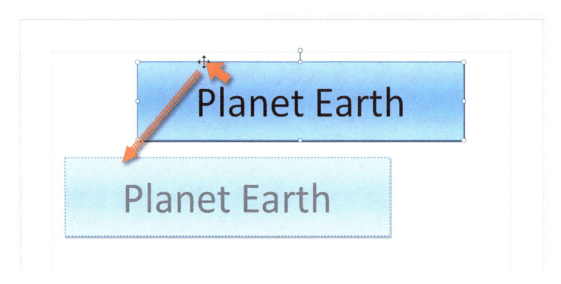

Resize Text Box

To resize a text box, click and drag one of the resize handles until the box is the desired size.

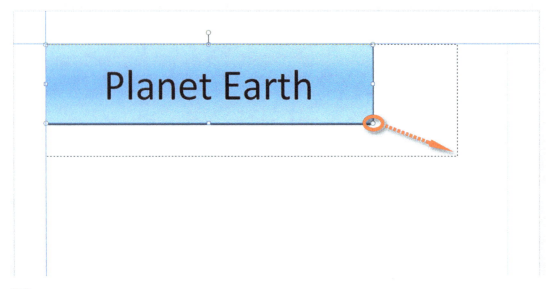

Rotate Text Box

To rotate a text box, click and drag the rotate handle on the top middle of the text box. Drag your mouse left or right to adjust rotation.

Text Direction

You can change the direction of the text in a text box. To rotate your text, select the text box, then from the 'text box tools' format ribbon, click 'text direction'.

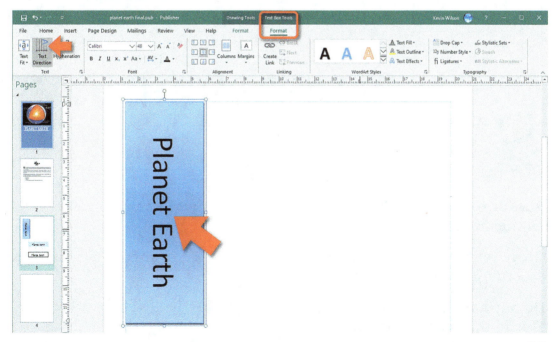

Text Autofit

You can automatically size and fit text inside your text boxes. To do this, select the text box you want to modify, then from the 'format' ribbon under 'text box tools', select 'text fit'.

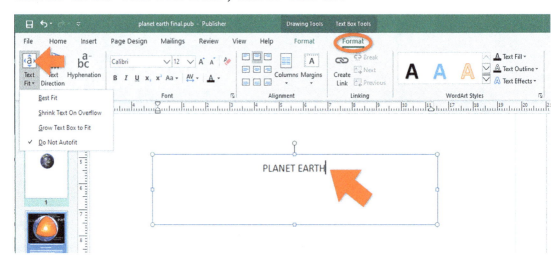

From the drop down menu, select an option.

Best fit makes the text larger or smaller to fit the text box.

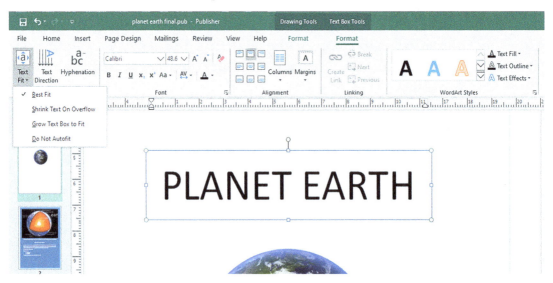

Shrink text on overflow automatically shrinks the text as you type to fill the size of the text box.

Grow text box to fit automatically increases the size of the text box according to the size of the text.

Do not autofit makes no automatic changes to the text or text box size. This is the default option.

Alignment

You can align your text inside your text box. You can align to the left, middle, right, top, middle or bottom. To do this, click your text box, then from the 'text box tools' format ribbon.

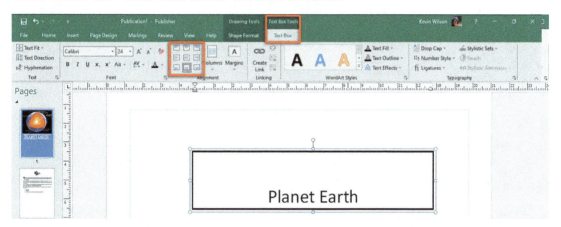

Select the alignment icon from the alignment section on the ribbon. For example, to put the text in the middle of the text box, select the middle icon.

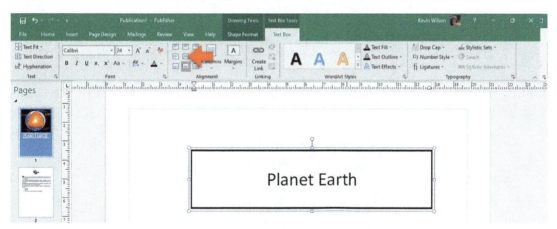

Line Spacing

To adjust the line spacing inside a text box, highlight the text. From your home ribbon, go to the 'paragraph' section and click the small arrow to the bottom right.

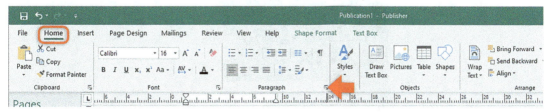

Chapter 3: Building a New Design

From the dialog box, select the 'indents & spacing' tab, go down to the 'line spacing' section and adjust the 'between lines' field.

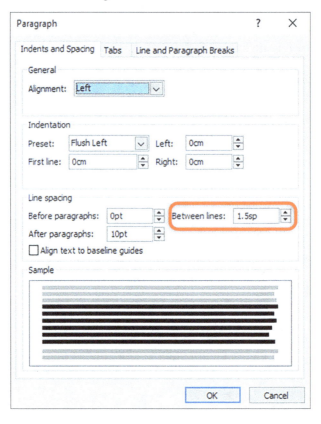

Click 'ok' when you're done. You can see below, the spacing between the lines of text.

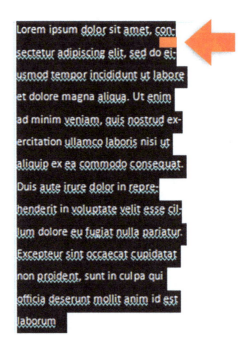

Connecting Text Boxes

As you work with text boxes, you might find that a text box isn't large enough to contain all of the text you want to include. When you run out of room for text, you can link the text boxes. Once two or more text boxes are connected, text will overflow or continue from one text box to the next. Select your text box. From the 'text box tools' format ribbon, click 'create link'.

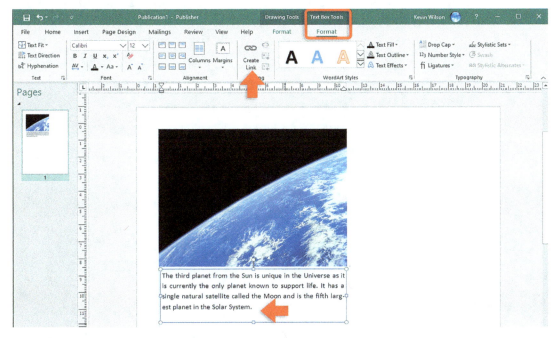

Your mouse pointer will turn into a 'link icon'. Click the position on your page where you want to link to.

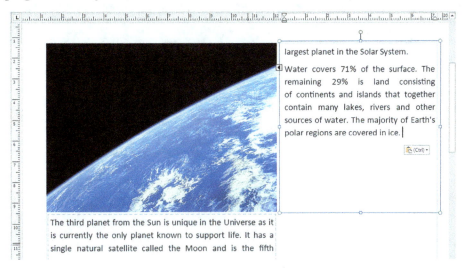

A new text box will appear. As you type your text, the text will flow onto the other text box.

Text Styles

Styles make it easier to keep the text formatting consistent throughout your publication.

A style is a preset with the typeface, font size and paragraph settings already defined. For example, you can have a paragraph style set to Calibri font, size 10, fully justified. This style could be called 'body text'.For your headings, you could have a paragraph style set to Arial black size 18. This can be called 'heading 1'. You can also have other subheadings such as heading 2 set to Arial black size14.

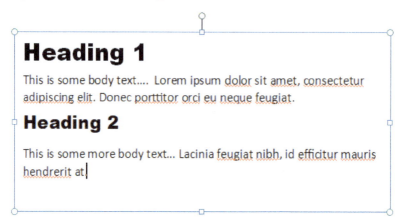

New Style

To create a new style, click 'styles' on the home ribbon tab, then select 'new style' from the drop down menu.

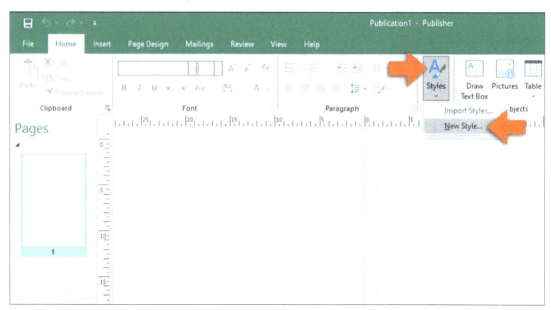

In the dialog box, in the field 'enter net style name', enter a name for your style, eg 'main title'.

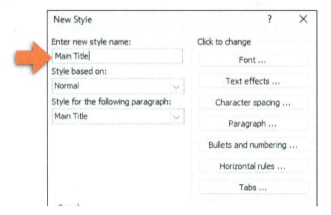

If you want to base the new style on an existing style, select a style from the 'style based on' field.

If you want to automatically switch to a style after you press enter when using this style, select it in the 'style for the following paragraph'. For example, if this is a heading style, you can automatically change to body text when you press enter after typing in a heading.

On the right hand side of the dialog box run through the 'click to change' section, so set the font, text effects, character spacing, paragraph spacing, bullets and numbering, horizontal rules, or tabs.

Click on 'fonts'. In the dialog box that appears, select the font, style, color, and size you want to assign to this paragraph style. You can also add other text effects underneath. Click ok when you're done.

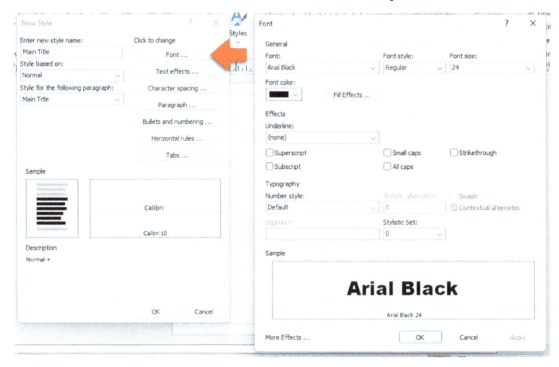

Click 'text effects' to change transparency, shadows, outlines etc. Click 'character spacing' to change the tracking and kerning of the text. Click 'paragraph' to change the spacing between paragraphs, tabs and indentations. Click 'bullets and numbering' to change the style of lists creating using this style. Click 'horizontal rules' to add a line before or after the style. Click on 'tabs' to assign tab stops for this style.

Update Style

To re-define or update a style, first select the text, then apply the font typeface and size, etc.

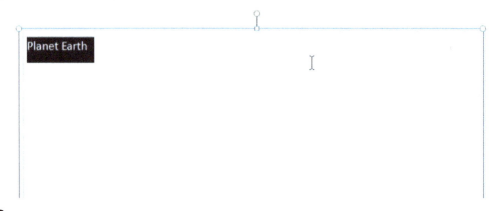

From the home ribbon, click on 'styles'. Scroll down the list, then righ click on the style you want to assign the selected style to. In this example, I'm going to assign the style of the selected text to 'heading 1'. So I'd right click on 'heading 1', then select 'update to match selection'.

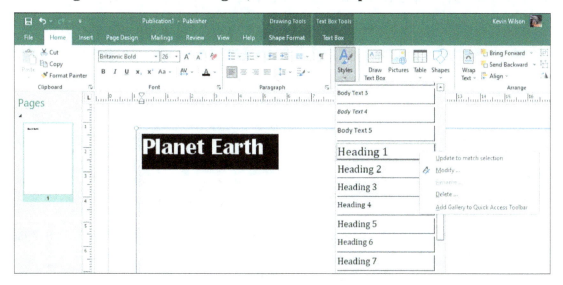

Apply Style

To apply a style to your publication, highlight the text you want to apply the style to, then from the home ribbon click 'styles'.

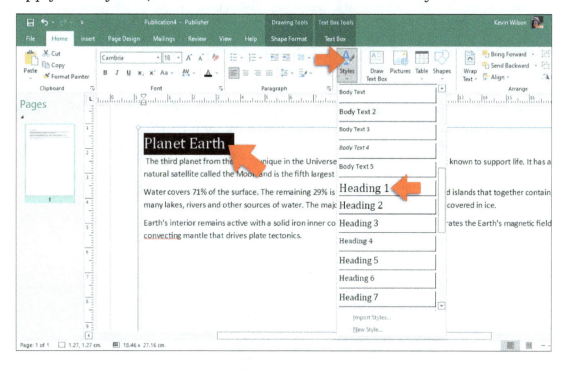

Scroll down the list, click on the style you want to apply.

Tables

We have added some more text about world population to our document. Now we want to add a table to illustrate our text.

To insert a table, go to your insert ribbon and select table.

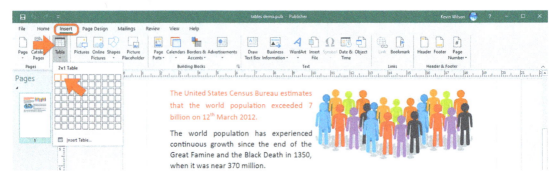

In the grid that appears highlight the number of rows and columns you want. For this table, 1 row and 2 columns.

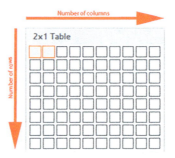

This will add a table with 1 row & 2 columns to your document.

Drag the table into position and enter your data. To move between cells on the table press the tab key. When you get to the end of the row, pressing tab will insert a new row.

Total annual births were highest in the late 1980s at about 139 million and is now expected to remain essentially constant at their 2011 level of 135 million, while deaths number 56 million per year, and are expected to increase to 80 million per year by 2040.

Country	Population
China	1,372,000,000
India	1,276,900,000
USA	321,793,000
Indonesia	252,164,800
Brazil	204,878,000

Resize Table

To resize a table, click and drag one of the corners of the grey border.

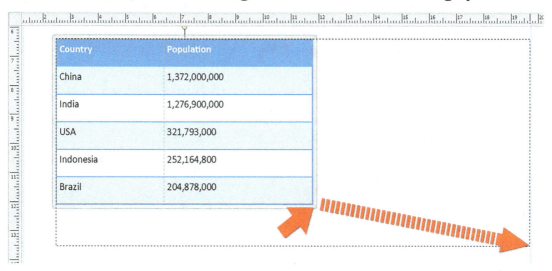

Move Table

To move your table, click anywhere on the table, then click and drag the grey border.

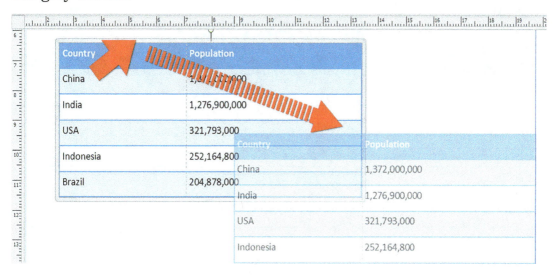

Formatting Tables

When you click on a table in your document, two new ribbons appear under 'table tools': design and layout.

The design ribbon allows you to select pre-set designs for your table, such as column and row shading, borders, and color.

In the centre of your design ribbon, you'll see a list of designs. Click the small arrow on the bottom right of the 'table styles' panel to open it up.

For this table, I am going to choose one with blue headings and shaded rows.

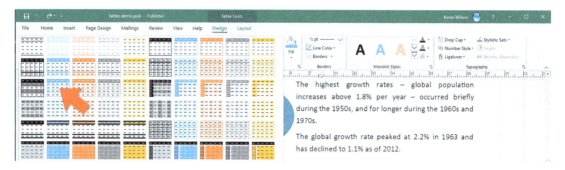

Add a Column

You can add a column to the right hand side of the table. To do this, click in the end column.

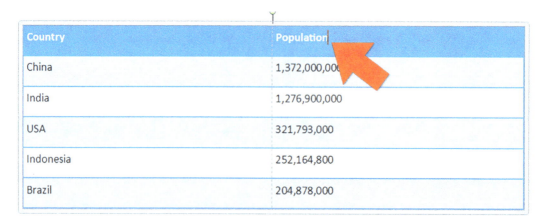

Select the layout ribbon under 'table tools', and select 'insert right'.

This inserts a column to the right of the one you selected. Resize your table if needed.

74

Insert a Row

To add a row, click on the row where you want to insert. For example, I want to add a row between USA and Indonesia. So click on Indonesia, as shown below.

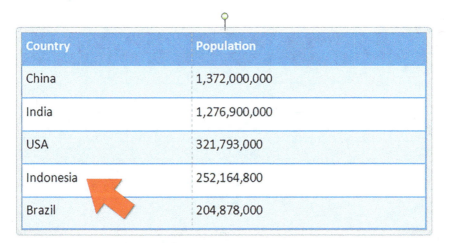

Select the layout ribbon from the table tools section.

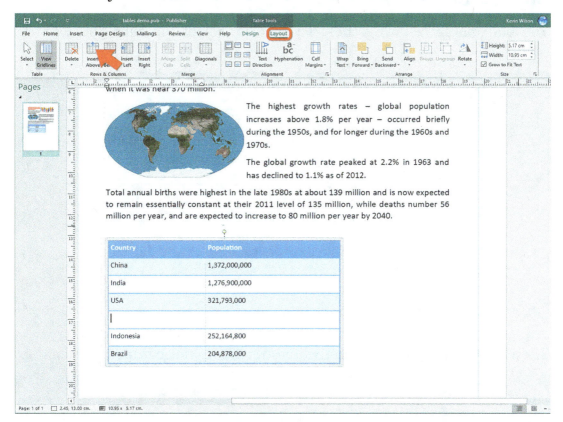

Click 'insert above'. This will insert a row above the one you selected earlier.

Resizing Rows & Columns

You can resize the column or row by clicking and dragging the row or column dividing line to the size you want.

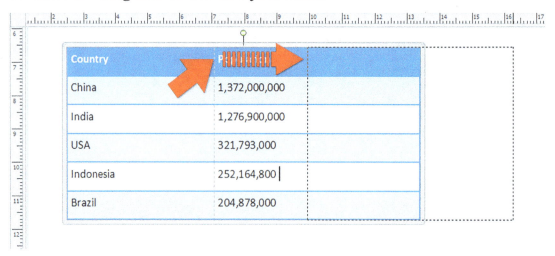

Merge Cells

You can merge cells together. To do this, select the cells you want to merge.

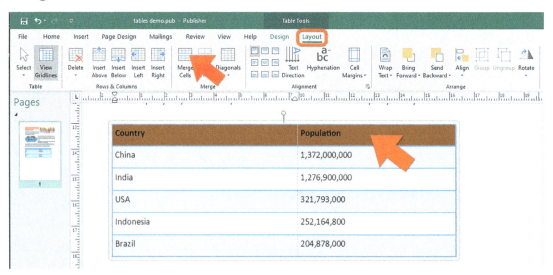

Then select 'merge cells' from the layout ribbon in the table tools section.

All the selected cells will be merged into a single cell.

Align Cell Text

You can change text alignment in the cells of the table. To do this, select the cells you want to align. Click and drag...

Country	Population	Percentage of World
China	1,372,000,000	18.5
India	1,276,900,000	17.5
USA	321,793,000	4.35
Indonesia	252,164,800	3.35
Brazil	204,878,000	2.77

Select the layout ribbon in the table tools section, as shown below.

From the alignment section, use the nine boxes to select the text alignment you want to apply to the cells.

Here's a quick guide to what the 9 different alignments look like. In the diagram below, note where each box on the left puts the text in the cells in the example on the right.

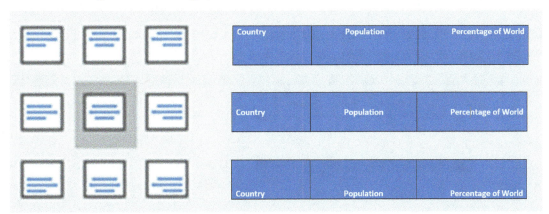

For example, select the center box to align the cells to the middle of the cell.

Cell Border

Select the cells you want to add a border to.

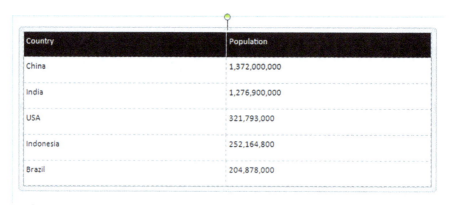

Click the 'table tools' design tab. Select a line thickness

Select a line color

Click 'borders'. From the drop down, select where on your selection you want the borders to appear.

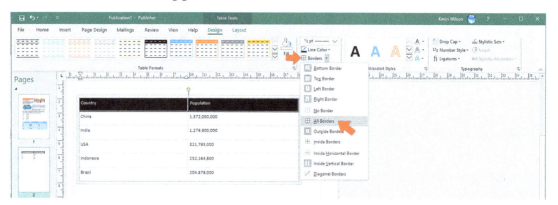

Cell Color

Select the cell or cells you want to change color

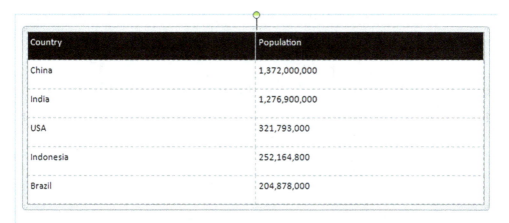

Click 'table tools' design tab.

Click the fill. Select a color from the pallet.

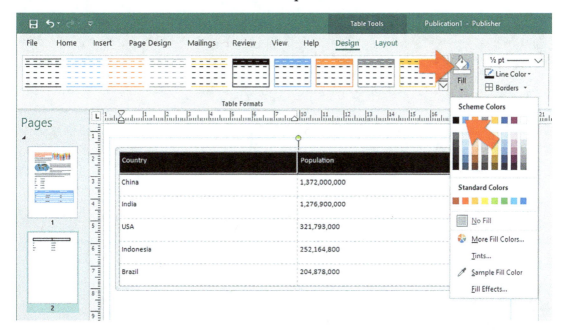

Text Direction

Also you can arrange the text vertically, this usually works well for headings.

To do this, select the heading rows in your table.

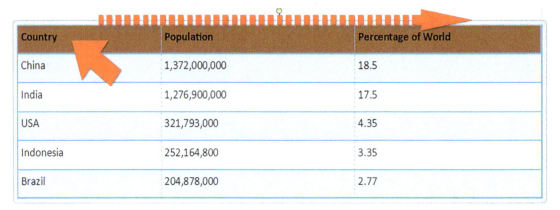

From the layout ribbon click 'text direction'.

Here, you can see the direction of the selected text has changed to vertical.

Border Art

Border Art allows you to add fancy, pre-designed borders to your pages

To use Border Art, select your page, then from the 'home' ribbon select 'shapes'. From the drop down, select a rectangle.

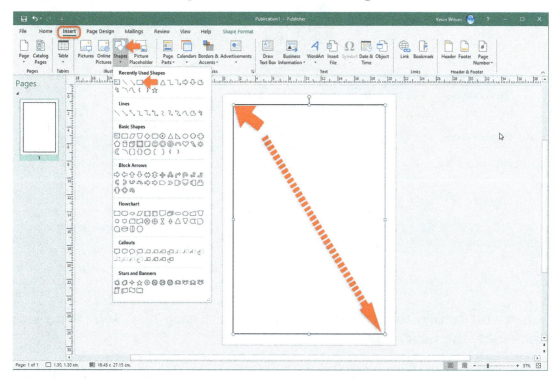

Click and drag the shape to create the page border.

Right-click on the border, select 'format autoshape' from the menu. Select the 'colors and lines' tab, and then click 'border art'.

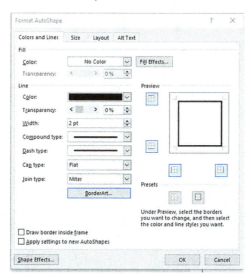

In the Available Borders list, click the border you want, and then click 'ok'.

When you return to the 'format autoshape' dialog box, select the size and color, then click 'ok'.

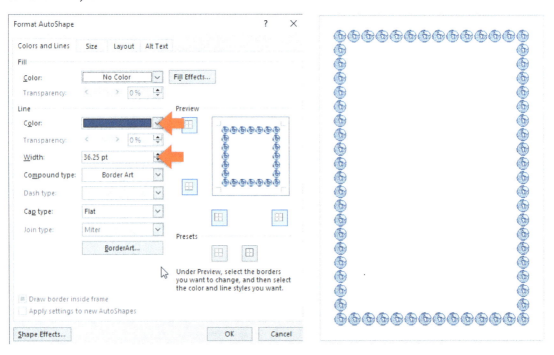

Your border around the rectangle you added will change

Layout Guides

Guides is a feature designed to help you to align objects in a publication. Publisher contains various layout guides you can use to make your publication look more consistent and professional.

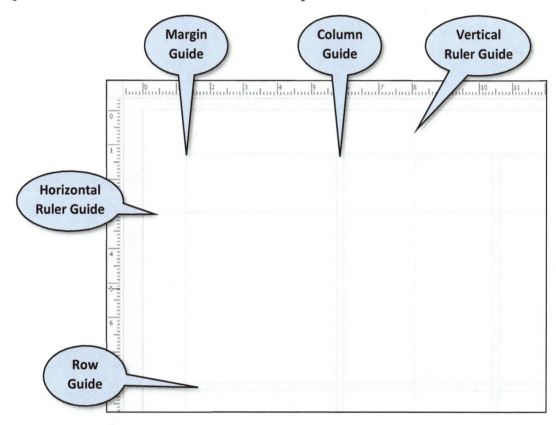

You can set up guides on each individual page, or on your master page. See page 93 for more information on creating a master page.

Preset Guides

Publisher comes with some common preset layout guides and grids. Graphic designers use these grids to keep their designs consistent.

To find the grid layouts, click on the layout ribbon tab, then select layouts.

Here, you can select from a number of built in guides.

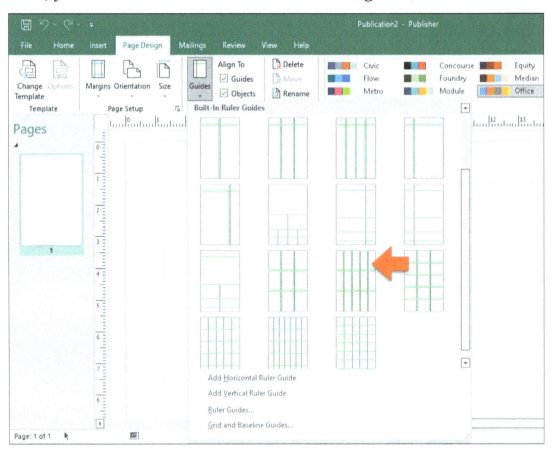

For example, if you were designing a newsletter or newspaper, the design is split into columns usually five or six depending on the size of the paper. Let's use 5 columns as we're using an A4 sheet of paper.

Look across the page and you can clearly see each column.

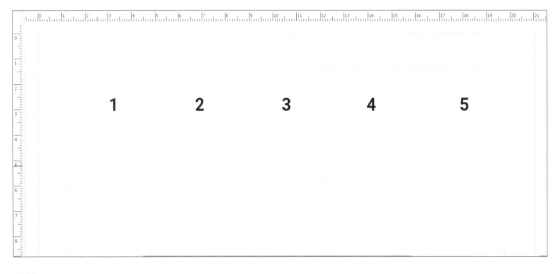

Each column is aligned to the grid. Here we have some text boxes containing the main story with a photograph placed in one of the columns.

Creating Row & Column Guides

To create your own rows and column guides, click the page design ribbon tab then select guides. From the drop down menu, select 'grid and baseline guides'.

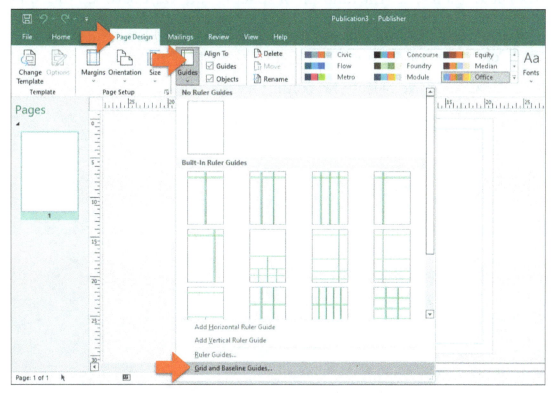

Click the Grid Guides tab. Under column guides, enter the number of columns that you want in the columns field. Then enter the amount of spacing you want between the columns in the spacing field.

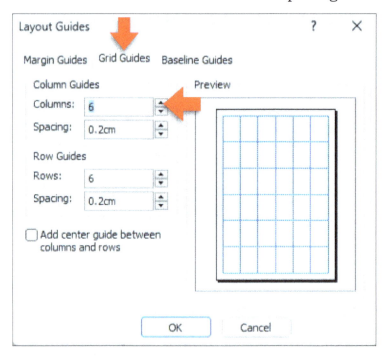

Do the same for rows. Enter the number of rows that you want in the rows field, then enter the amount of spacing you want between the rows in the spacing field. Add 'center guide between columns and rows' adds a marker in the center of the space between the rows and columns. Click 'ok' when you're done.

In this example, we selected 6 columns and 6 rows.

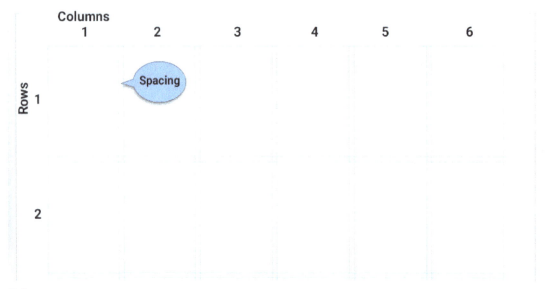

Creating a Vertical Ruler Guide

You can create guide lines to help you align the elements on your design. To do this, click either the horizontal or vertical ruler. Then drag your mouse pointer to the position on your page.

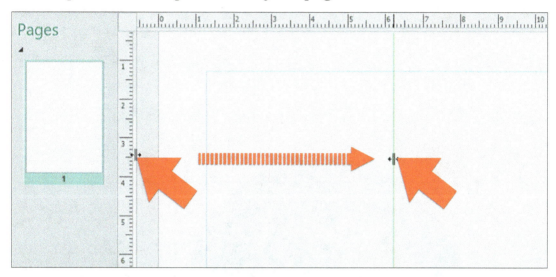

Click and drag the guide to move it again if you need to. This helps you to line things up within your publication.

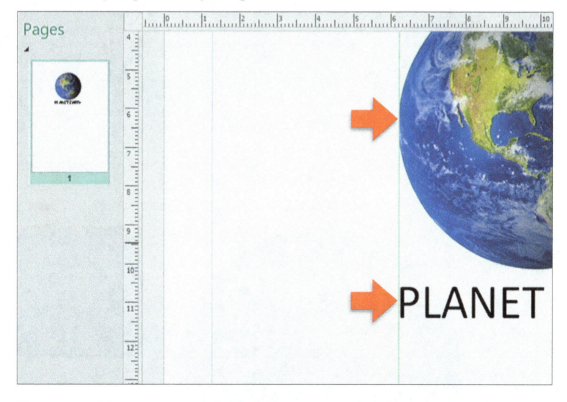

You can add as many vertical guides as you need.

Creating a Horizontal Ruler Guide

You can do the same with the top margin. Click and drag the margin down to the position you want.

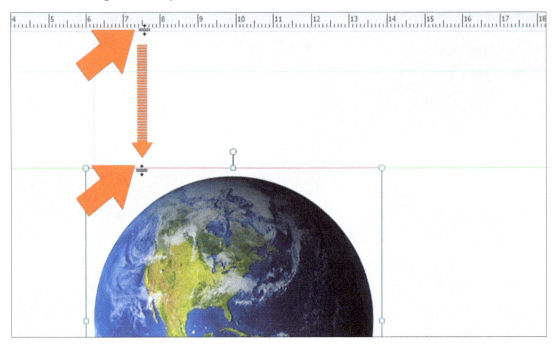

Now you can align objects

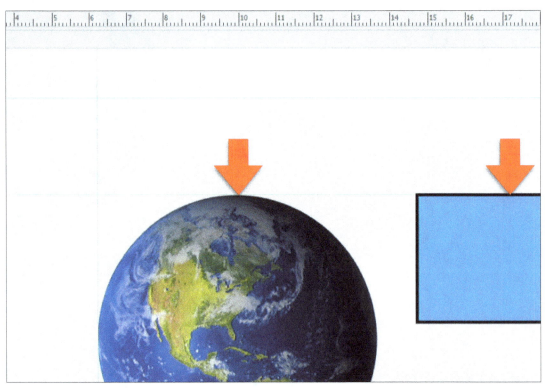

Baseline Guides

Baseline guides help you to align text that is not linked between text boxes in the columns of your design.

Click on the page design ribbon tab, then select guides. From the drop down menu, select 'grid and baseline guides'.

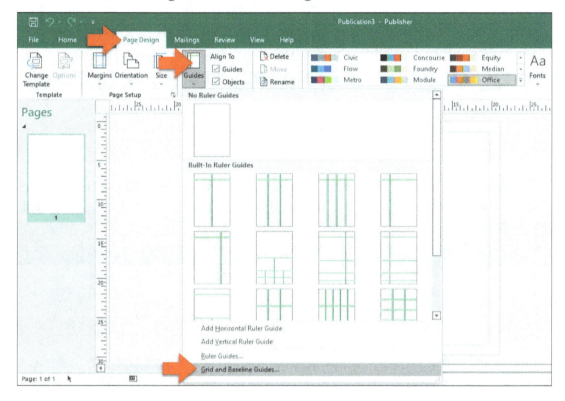

Click the 'baseline guides' tab.

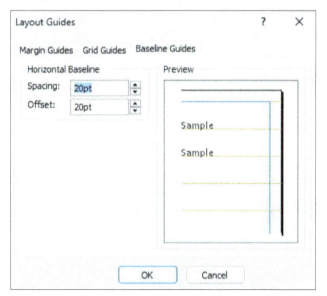

Chapter 3: Building a New Design

In the spacing box field, increase or decrease the amount of spacing between each baseline. In the offset field, adjust the amount of spacing between the top margin and the first baseline guide.

To show the baseline guides on the page, select the view ribbon tab, then in the 'show' section, click on 'baselines'.

You can turn the text alignment on or off in a text box. To do this, select the text box, then from the home ribbon tab, select the 'paragraph settings' icon.

Select the indents and spacing tab. Click on 'align text to baseline guides'.

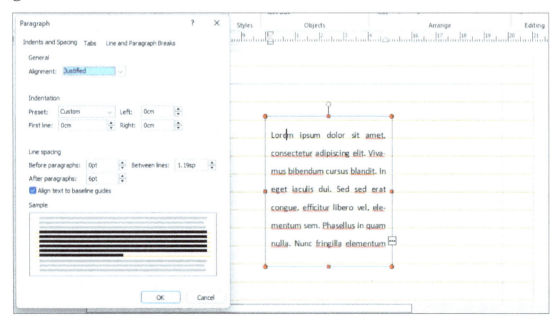

Exercises

1. Open a new publication.

2. Insert a textbox, then enter some text

Planet Earth

3. Add a border to the text box

Planet Earth

4. Shade the textbox with dark blue

Planet Earth

5. Change the color of the text to white

Planet Earth

6. Change the font of the text

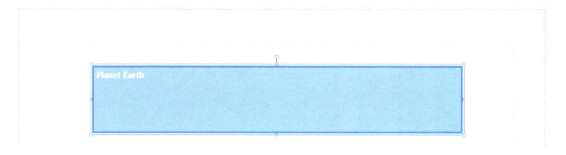

7. Change the text size of the font

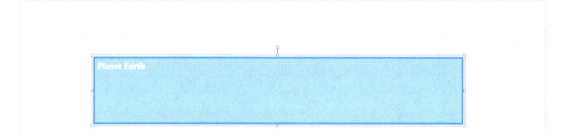

8. Change the first word to bold and align the text in the textbox to centred

9. Insert a table with three columns and three rows

10.　Shade the top row in light blue

11.　Add a table border

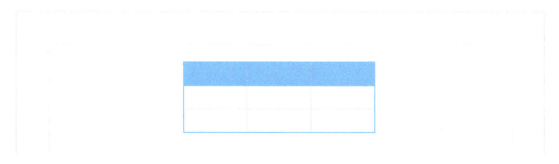

12. Enter some headings into the table

13. Enter some data into the table cells

14. Format the table headings

15. Change the table headings to white text and center them

Language	Speakers	
Chinese	1.1 Billion	
English	340 million	
Spanish	322 Million	

16. Add a vertical guide half way across the page.

17. Add a horizontal guide half way down the page.

18. Add a layout grid with 9 columns.

19. Adjust the layout grid to include 9 rows

4

Working with Pages

When you create a publication, Publisher applies some default settings depending on what options you selected when you created the publication. This could be page size, orientation, margins, number of pages and so on.

Pages are usually designed as a single page such as a flyer or as part of a multi-page spread such as a booklet.

In this chapter, we'll take a look at page structure, layout and page masters.

Check out the video resources. Open your browser and navigate to:

elluminetpress.com/pub-pages

For this section you'll need the files from:

elluminetpress.com/ms-pub

Scroll down to the file resources section and download the files.

Page View

Using the view ribbon tab, you can change the page view. Here you can zoom the page to show the whole thing or zoom to the page width.

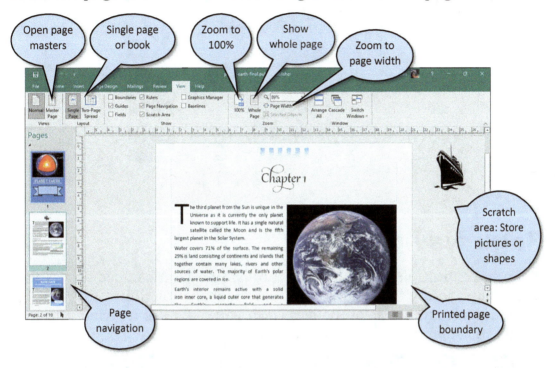

If you zoom out, you'll see the scratch area, sometimes also called the paste board. This is where you can put any images or shapes you aren't currently using. You can drag the images from the scratch area into your publication pages. Or you can drag the image off your publication into the scratch area.

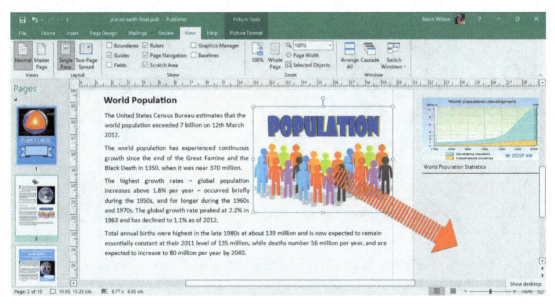

You can also view your publication as a single page, or as a booklet. To do this, select 'two-page view' from the view ribbon tab.

Page Navigation

If you have multiple pages in your publication, you can see an index of these pages using the page navigation sidebar. You'll find this sidebar along the left hand side of the screen. If you don't see it, select the view ribbon tab then click on 'page navigation'.

Just click on a page in the navigation sidebar to jump to that page. To move a page, click and drag the thumbnail to another position.

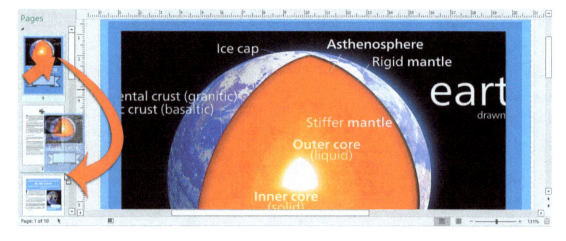

If you want to delete a page, right click on the page then select 'delete' from the popup menu.

Publication Pages

You can add pages or duplicate a page in your publication.

Adding

If you want to add a page, select the insert ribbon tab, then click on 'page'.

From the drop down menu select 'insert blank page'. This will add a page after the current page (or the page selected in the page navigation sidebar).

If you want to add more than one, select 'insert pages'. In the dialog box, enter the number of pages, select whether you want the page to be inserted before or after the current page.

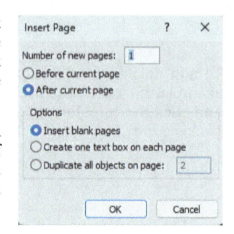

Under options, select whether you want a blank page, or a page with a textbox, or if you want the page to contain objects such as textboxes or images from a certain page you've already created.

Duplicating

To duplicate a page, right click on the page in the page navigation sidebar on the left, then select 'insert duplicate page'.

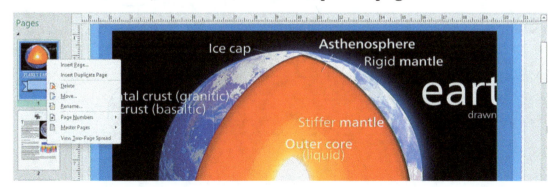

Page Background

You can change the color of the page. You can also add a gradient, a texture or an image.

To do this, from the 'page design' ribbon tab, click on 'background'. Select a pre-defined solid or gradient background from the samples.

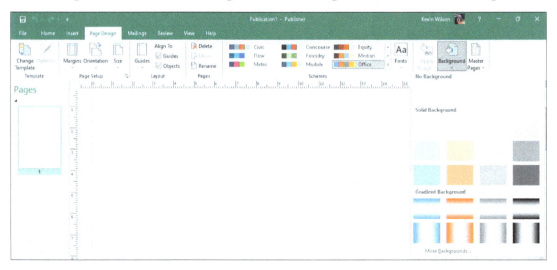

To add an image or create your own, select 'more backgrounds'. For example, if I wanted to create a gradient that goes from white to blue and back to white, I could do this with gradient stops. From the 'format background' dialog box, select 'gradient fill'.

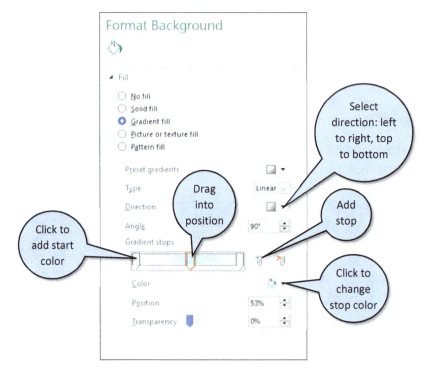

Click on the left gradient stop and select your first color - the color you want the gradient to start with, eg white.

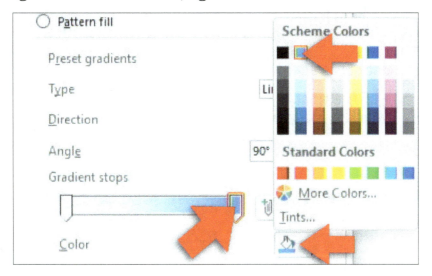

Click on the right gradient stop, select the color you want to end the gradient with, eg, blue.

If you want to use an image, select 'picture or texture fill' from the 'format background' dialog box we saw earlier.

Click 'insert' under 'picture source', then select the image you want to use.

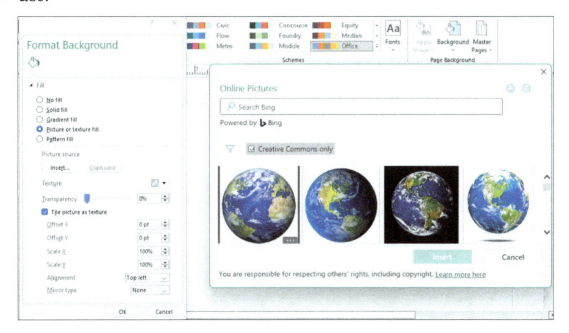

Set the transparency to about 70 or 80% if you want it to appear as a watermark in the background.

Page Masters

Page Masters allow you to repeat design and layout elements on multiple pages in a publication. This creates a more consistent appearance throughout your work and allows you to update the design in one place, rather than changing them on each page.

Editing Master Pages

For example, if you are creating a booklet, you can add page headers or page numbers to each page.

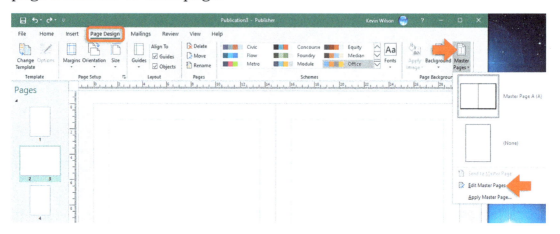

Add a header such as a title.

Add a footer. Click on the footer of the page.

Add a page number, click 'insert page number'.

Creating Master Pages

To create a new master, select the 'page design' ribbon tab, then click 'add master page'.

Give the master a descriptive name in the 'description' field. Click 'ok'.

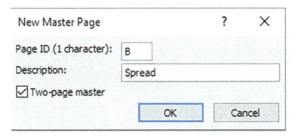

If you want the master to be a two page spread, one you'd find in the middle of a booklet, click 'two-page master'. If you just want an individual page, un-tick this option.

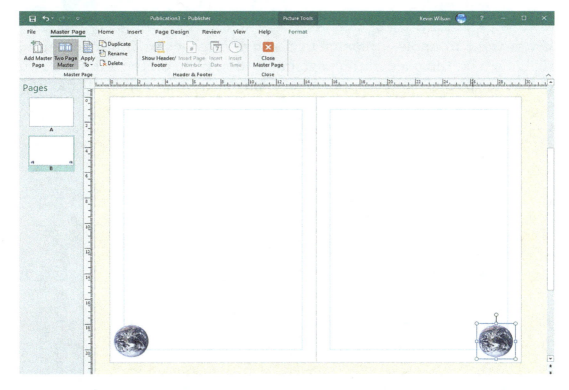

Now, build your master. You can insert pictures or text boxes as normal using the 'insert' ribbon tab.

Applying Masters

To apply a master to a page, right click on the page or spread in the page navigation pane on the left hand side. Go down to 'master pages' and select a master from the slideout menu.

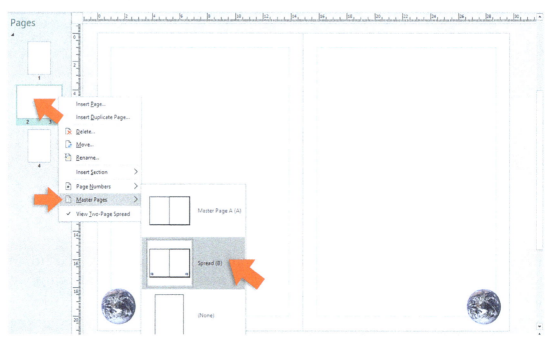

If you want to apply a master to a range of pages or multiple pages, right click on the page in the page navigation pane on the left. Go down to 'master pages', select 'apply master pages' from the slideout menu.

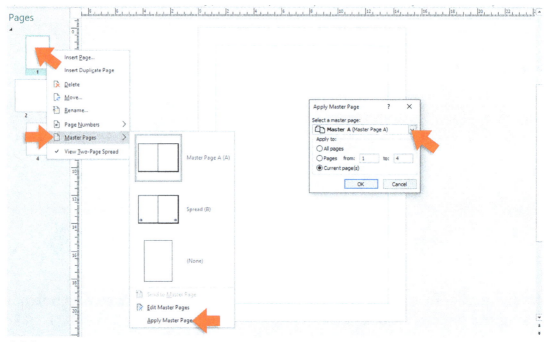

From the dialog box, select the master you want to apply

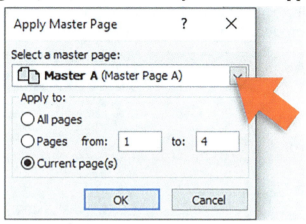

Select which pages want to apply the master to, eg 'all pages'. Click 'ok'.

Margins

Many domestic and office printers don't print to the very edge of the page, instead they have a printable area about a half-inch around the edge of the paper.

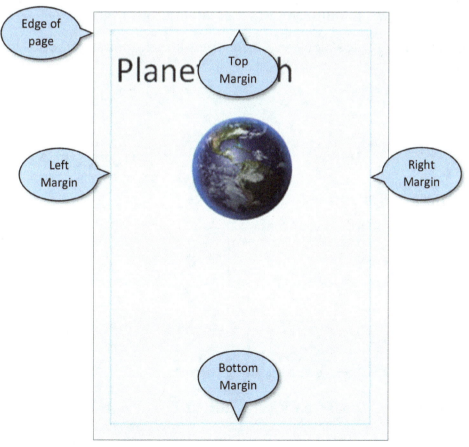

Chapter 4: Working with Pages

You'll find your margins on the page design ribbon tab. Click on 'margins'. In the drop down menu, you can select from some preset margins: wide, moderate, narrow, or none.

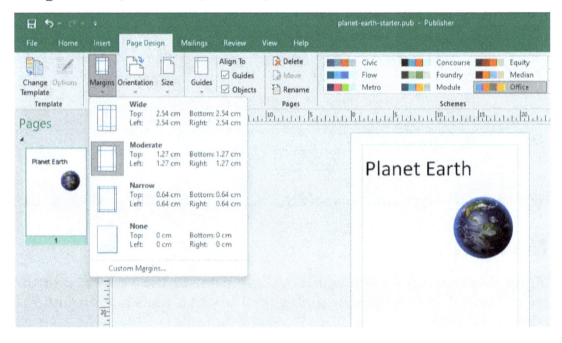

To enter you own measurements, select 'custom margins'.

Under 'margin guides' section, enter the margin measurements for your printer.

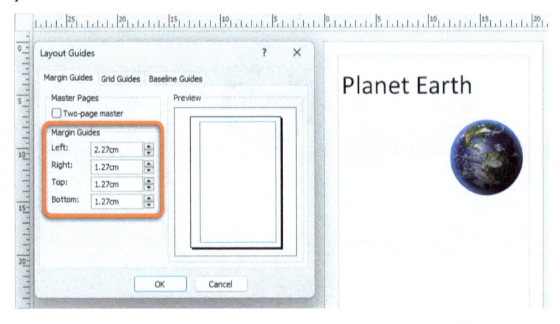

The margin will appear as a blue dotted box around the edges of the page.

Multipage Publications

Multi-page publications include a range of printed or digital materials that span several pages such as:

- Books including fiction, non-fiction, educational materials, and manuals.

- Magazines and Journals containing articles, features, and advertisements.

- Brochures and Catalogs for marketing purposes, showcasing products, services, or company information.

- Reports and Manuals to provide detailed information or instructions, such as annual reports, technical manuals, and policy guides.

- Newsletters released by organizations or communities to update their members or customers.

Creating a Spread

Creating a spread in a publication, such as in a magazine or newsletter, typically involves designing two facing pages side by side.

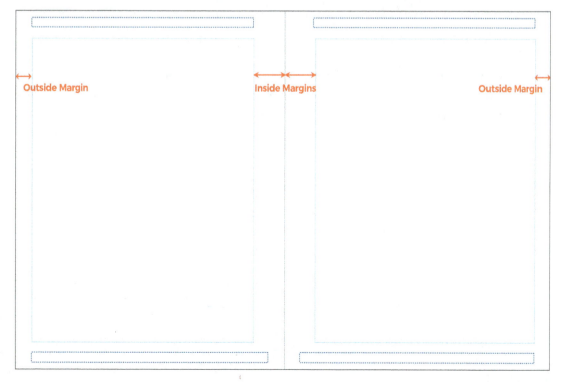

Chapter 4: Working with Pages

In the example below, I have created a newsletter that is 3 pages long and is going to be in a booklet.

From the 'view' ribbon tab click on 'master page'.

On the 'master page' ribbon tab, select 'two page master'.

Click 'apply to'. Select 'all pages' from the drop down menu.

Next, we want to set the inside margins so the text doesn't print too close to the bind side of the page. To do this, click on the 'page design' ribbon tab. In the 'page setup' section, click 'margins', then select 'custom margins'. Increase the 'inside' margin setting, eg 2.5cm from the edge

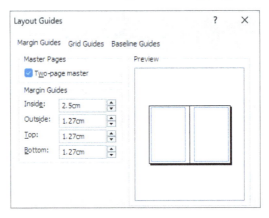

Click 'ok'.

Click back on the 'page master' ribbon tab, then click 'close master page'.

To view the publication as a spread, click on the 'two page spread' icon on the bottom right of the status bar.

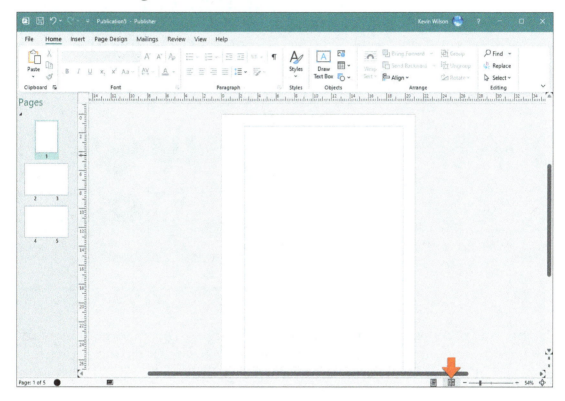

Now, when you add pages, you'll notice they are added as a spread ie two pages side by side.Focus on each page separately. You can use different layouts, styles, and content on each page without worrying about how they will interact with the opposite page. Make sure you align your text and graphics to the margin line.

Before finalizing your work, use the 'Print Preview' option to see how each page will look when printed, especially if your publication will be printed and distributed using a domestic or office printer.

To do this select 'file' on the top left, then click on 'print.

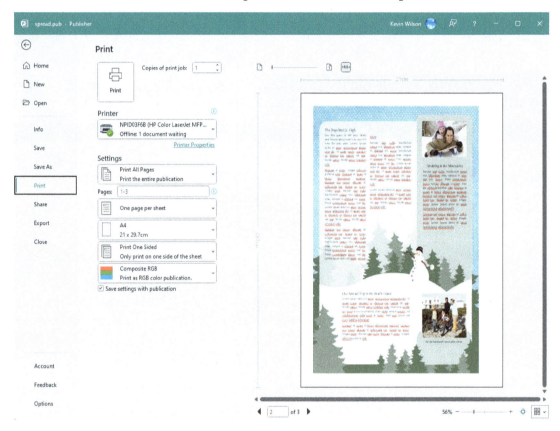

Using the panel of settings on the left, choose the printer you want to use from a list of available printers. This includes local printers connected to your computer and network printers.

Set the number of copies you want to print.

Select Print One-Sided. This prints on only one side of each sheet of paper.

Over on the right of the screen you'll see a preview of how your publication will look when printed, based on the current settings. This is useful for checking the layout and ensuring everything is correctly aligned before printing.

If you intend to use a commercial print service, export as a PDF. See page 188.

Exercises

1. Create a new publication

2. Create a master page

3. Add a page header on the top right of the page

4. Add the page numbers to the bottom right corner.

5. Apply your new master to the pages in your document.

5

Adding Graphics

You can add images, shapes and other objects to your publication.

In this chapter, we'll take a look at

- Adding Images
- Adding Clipart
- Adding Effects to Images
- Cropping Images
- Adjusting Images
- Wrap Text around Image
- Adding Shapes
- Change Color
- Change Border
- Shadow
- Page Parts
- Borders & Accents
- Calendars
- Advertisements
- WordArt
- Images Types

Check out the video resources. Open your browser and navigate to

elluminetpress.com/pub-graphics

For this section you'll need the files from:

elluminetpress.com/ms-pub

Scroll down to the files section and download the files.

Adding Images

Adding images to your document is easy.

There are two ways.

- Your own photos and pictures stored on your computer or OneDrive.

- Clipart. This is a large library of images that can be used in your documents.

Go to your 'insert' ribbon and click on 'Pictures'

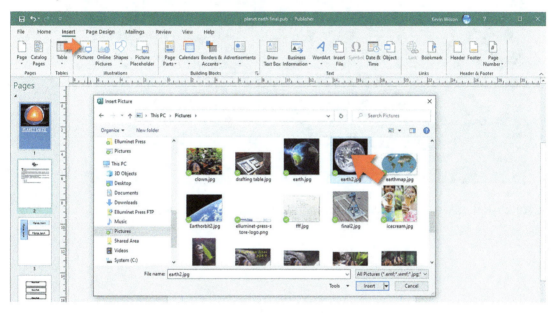

Choose the picture or photo you want from the dialog box that appears. Click insert.

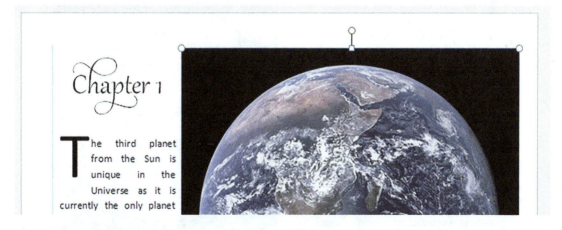

This will insert your photo into your document.

Chapter 5: Adding Graphics

Once imported into Publisher, you may need to resize the image, as sometimes they can come in a bit big. To do this click on the image, you'll see small handles appear on each corner of the image. These are called resize handles. You can use them by clicking and dragging a corner toward the centre of the image to make it smaller as shown below. Hold down the shift key as you resize the image to prevent it from being distorted.

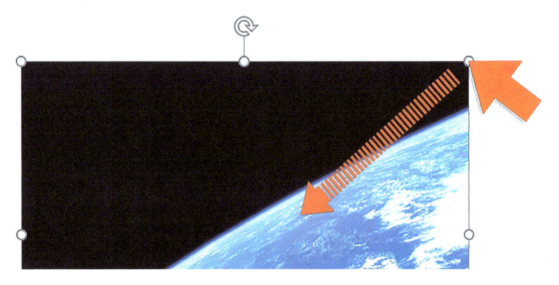

Click and drag the photo into position on your document.

Images from Google

You can also search for images on Google. *If you do this, make sure you only source images from the public domain, creative commons or a stock photo site. Don't steal photos from other people's work.*

To download an image from Google, open your web browser and run a Google search, then select 'images'. From the 'usage rights' menu, select 'creative commons licenses'.

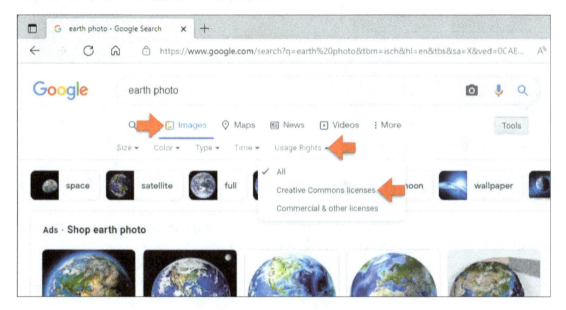

Scroll down the page, click on the image thumbnail in the search results, you'll see the image appear on the right of the screen. Right click the image.

Chapter 5: Adding Graphics

Select 'save image as' from the popup menu.

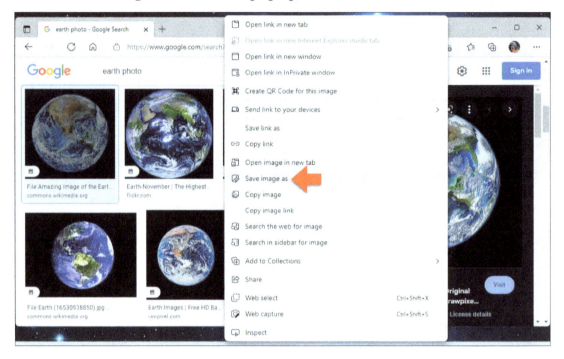

From the dialog box that appears, save the picture into your 'pictures' folder either on your PC or OneDrive folder.

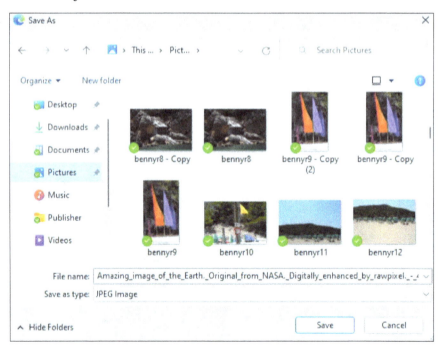

Once your image is saved into your pictures folder, you can import them into your publisher document using the same procedure at the beginning of the chapter.

Adding Clipart

Carrying on with our document, I want to add a new section called "World Population" and I want some clipart to illustrate this.

To add a clipart image, go to your insert ribbon and click 'online pictures'.

Then, in the dialog box, type in what you are looking for, as shown below. In this example, enter the search term 'population'.

In the search results, click the image you want then click insert.

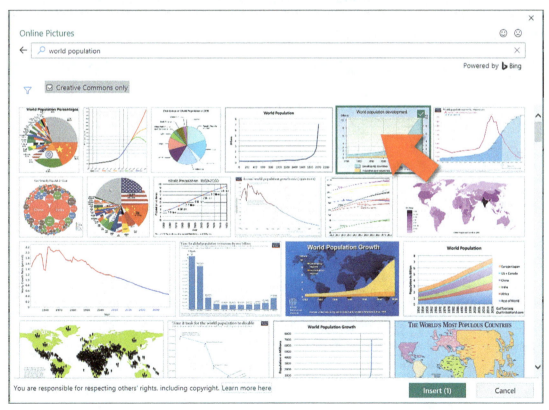

Again, you might need to resize and position the image. Hold down the shift key as you resize the image to prevent it from being distorted.

World Population

The United States Census Bureau estimates that the world population exceeded 7 billion on 12th March 2012.

The world population has experienced continuous growth since the end of the Great Famine and the Black Death in 1350, when it was near 370 million.

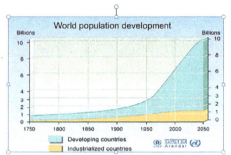

The highest growth rates – global population increases above 1.8% per year – occurred briefly during the 1950s, and for longer during the 1960s and 1970s. The global growth rate peaked at 2.2% in 1963 and has declined to 1.1% as of 2012.

Total annual births were highest in the late 1980s at about 139 million and is now expected to remain essentially constant at their 2011 level of 135 million, while deaths number 56 million per year, and are expected to increase to 80 million per year by 2040.

Adding Effects to Images

To add effects to your images, such as shadows and borders, click on your image, then select the 'picture tools' format b ribbon. In this example, click on the population image.

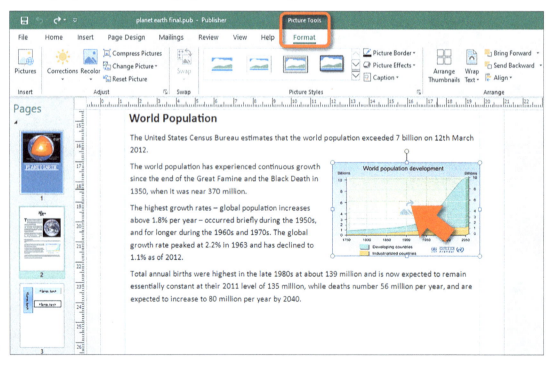

I want to create a nice reflection style to the image. To do this, click 'picture effects', then go down to 'reflection'. Select a variation as shown below.

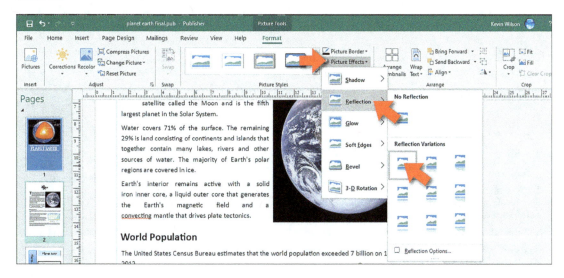

Try different effects, such as 'shadow', 'bevel' or 'glow'. See what effect they have...

Add a Caption

Click the image you want to add the caption to, then from the 'picture tools' format ribbon select 'caption'. From the drop down menu, select a caption style.

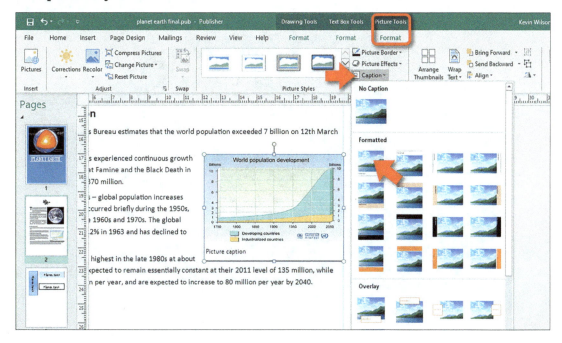

Type in your caption...

World Population

The United States Census Bureau estimates that the world population exceeded 7 billion on 12th March 2012.

The world population has experienced continuous growth since the end of the Great Famine and the Black Death in 1350, when it was near 370 million.

The highest growth rates – global population increases above 1.8% per year – occurred briefly during the 1950s, and for longer during the 1960s and 1970s. The global growth rate peaked at 2.2% in 1963 and has declined to 1.1% as of 2012.

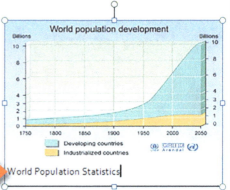

Total annual births were highest in the late 1980s at about 139 million and is now expected to remain essentially constant at their 2011 level of 135 million, while deaths number 56 million per year, and are expected to increase to 80 million per year by 2040.

Cropping Images

If you insert an image into your document, and it has unwanted parts, or you want to concentrate on one particular piece of the picture, you can crop the image

First, insert an image from your pictures library into your document.

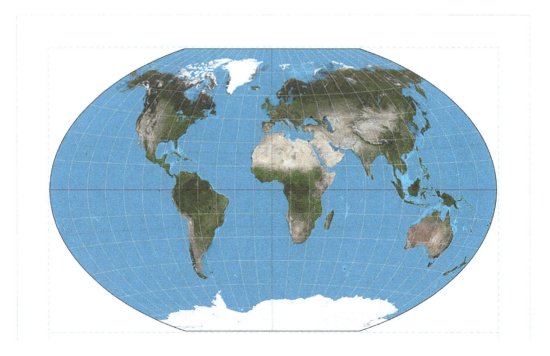

To crop, click on the image, then click the 'picture tools' format ribbon. From the format ribbon, click the crop icon.

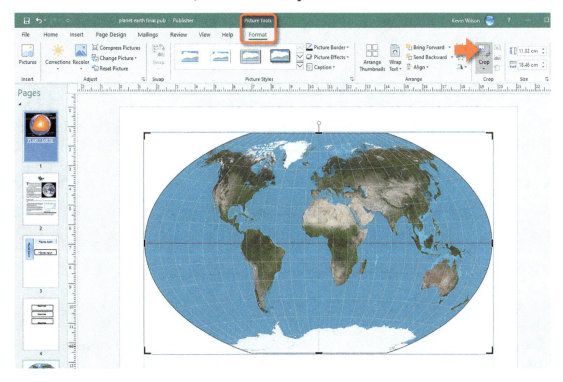

If you look closely at your image, you will see crop handles around the edges, shown circled below.

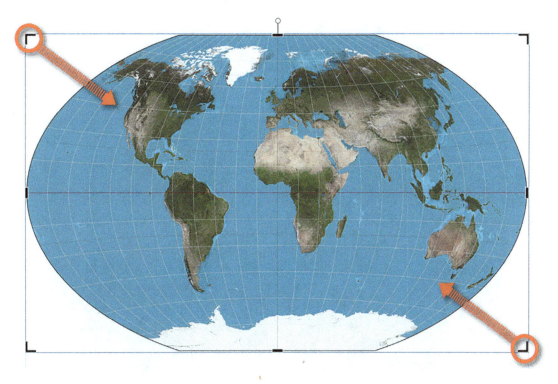

Click and drag these handles around the part of the image you want to keep. Eg, I just want to show Africa in the image.

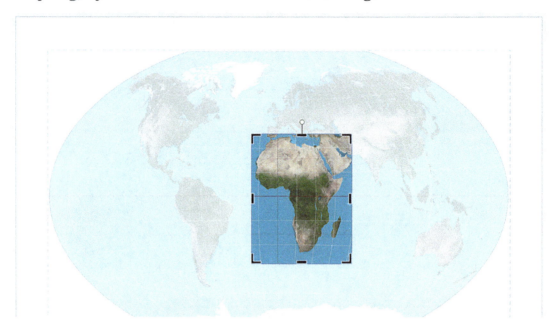

The light grey bits will be removed to leave the bit of the image inside the crop square. Click anywhere on your document to finish.

Crop to Shape

You can crop an image to fit inside a shape. First, insert an image from your pictures library into your document.

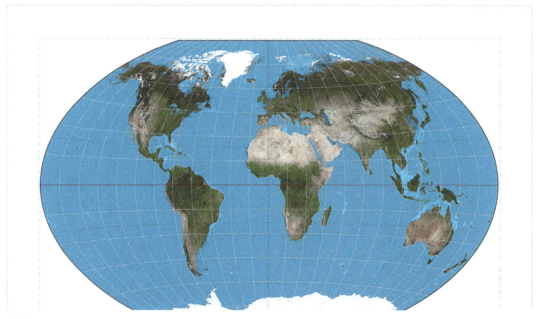

To crop, click on the image, then click the 'picture tools' format ribbon. From the format ribbon, click the down arrow under the crop icon. From the drop down menu, select 'crop to shape'.

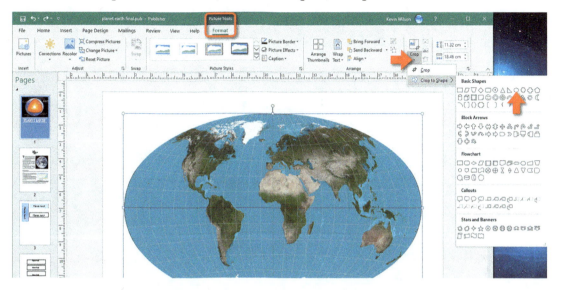

From the slideout, select a shape.

If you look closely at your image, you will see crop handles around the edges, shown circled below. Click and drag these handles around the part of the image you want to keep. Eg, I just want to show Africa in the image.

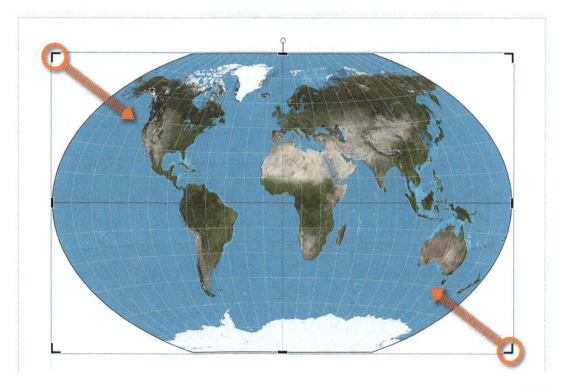

The light grey bits will be removed to leave the bit of the image inside the crop square. Click anywhere on your document to finish.

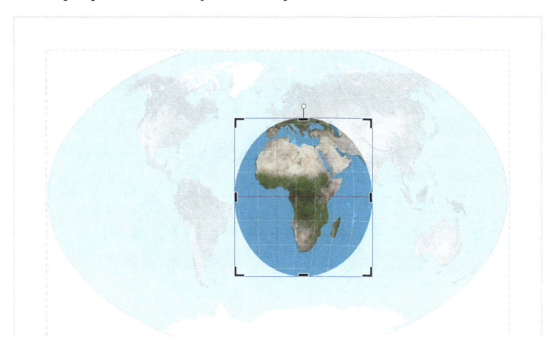

Adjusting Images

You can adjust the brightness and contrast of your images or re-color them so the image fits into your color scheme.

To adjust an image, first right click on it. From the popup menu select 'format picture'. From the dialog box, select the 'picture' tab.

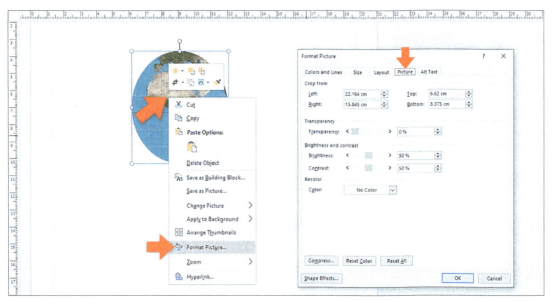

Now, use the transparency slider to change the transparency of the image. Use the brightness & contrast sliders to adjust the brightness and contrast. Use the recolor drop down to change the color of the image.

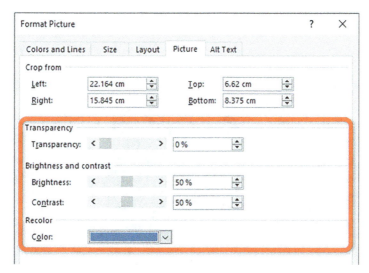

Click 'ok' when you're done.

Wrap Text around Images

When you insert an image, the image will be automatically wrapped with text, meaning the text will arrange itself around the image rather than underneath it or over it.

To change the text wrap, click on the image then from the format ribbon, click 'wrap text'.

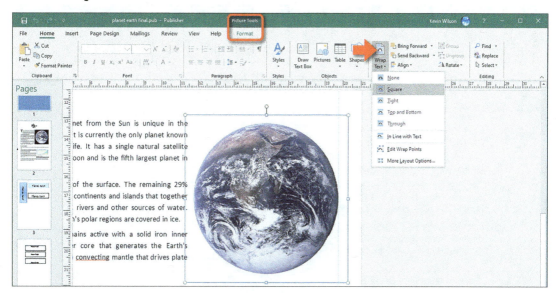

Select 'tight' from the drop down list to align the text squarely around the border of the image.

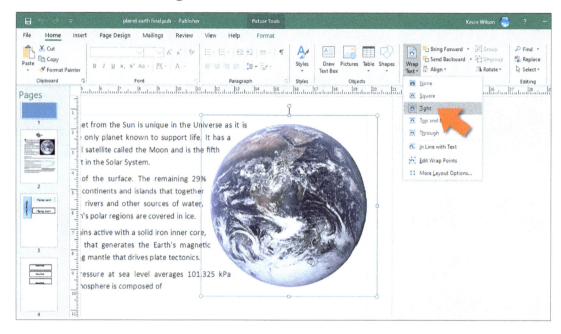

Click and drag the image into position if you need to. As you do this, you'll notice the text will arrange itself around the image.

Wrap Points

You can also customise the points at which the text wraps around the image. To do this, click the image then from the format ribbon, click 'wrap text'. Select 'edit wrap points' from the drop down menu.

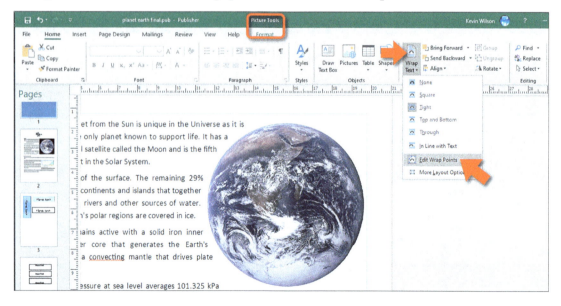

You'll see a dotted line appear around the image. This is called the wrap point. To edit, click and drag the dots.

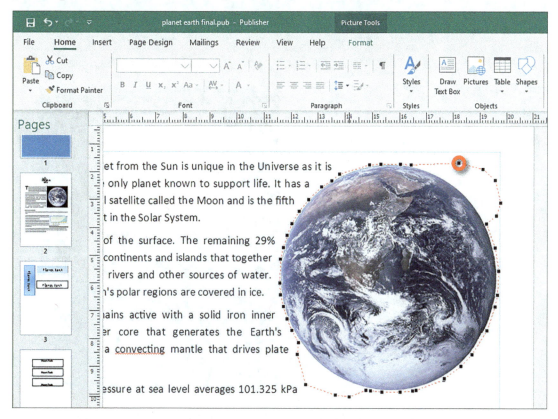

Adding Shapes

You can add various different shapes to your publication. You can add squares, rectangles, circles, lines, speech bubbles, as well as various flow chart symbols.

To insert a shape, select your 'insert' ribbon.

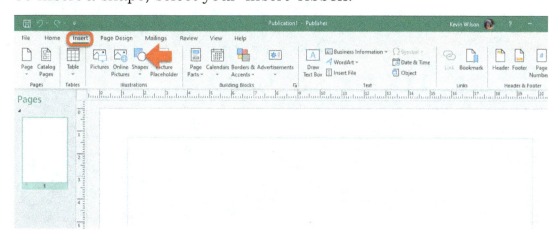

From the dropdown menu, select your shape.

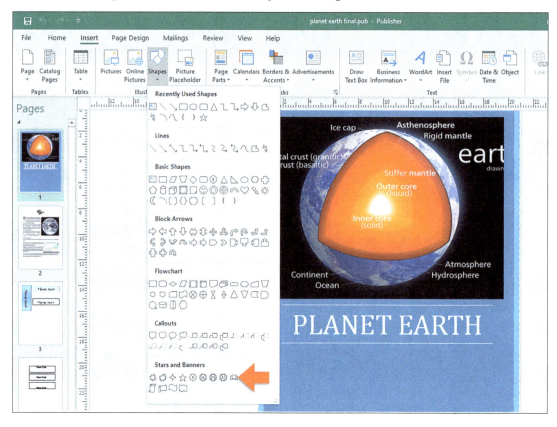

Click and drag your mouse on your document to create the shape.

Modifying Shapes

You can change the color, outline and add shadows to your shapes.

Change Color

To change this, click on your shape, then select the 'drawing tools' format ribbon.

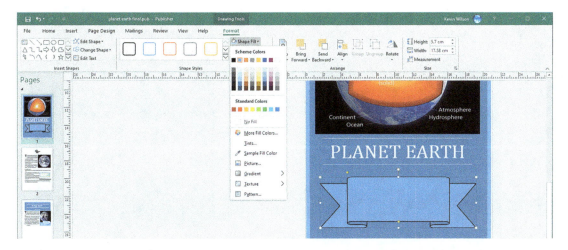

Select 'fill color', then select a color from the drop down menu.

If you want to add a gradient, select 'gradient' from the drop down menu. If you want to add a texture, select 'texture'.

Change Border

To change this, click on your shape, then select the 'drawing tools' format ribbon. Select 'shape outline', then select a color.

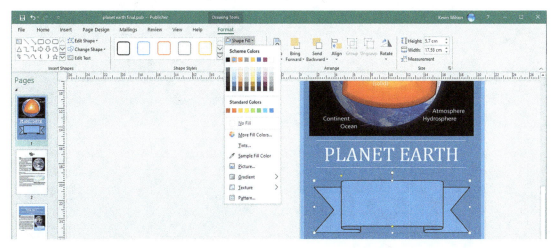

To change the thickness of the border, select 'weight'.

Add a Shadow

To add a shadow, click on your shape, then select the 'drawing tools' format ribbon.

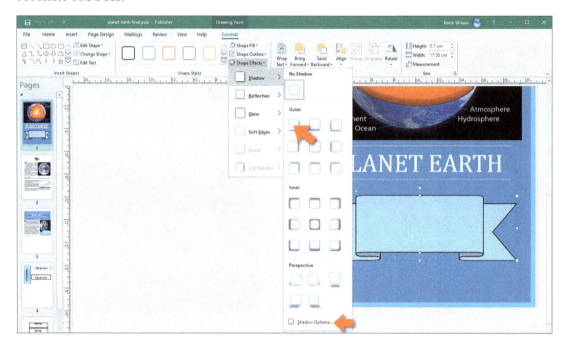

Select 'shape effects', then select an effect from the drop down menu.

To edit the effect, go down to '...options' at the bottom of the slideout menu.

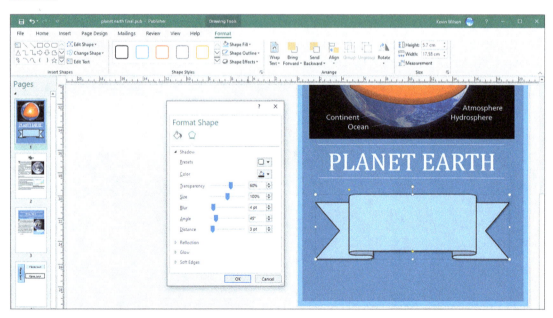

Use the sliders to customise your effect.

Align Objects

You can automatically align objects on your page. To do this, first select all the objects you want to align. Hold down the control key on your keyboard while you click the images you want to align.

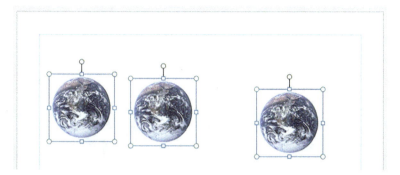

Click the 'picture tools' format ribbon and select 'arrange'. Click 'align'.

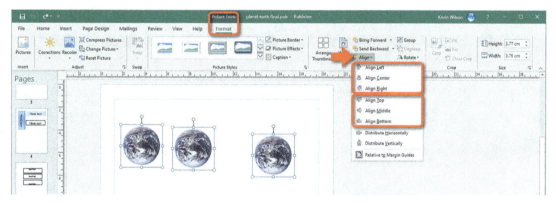

Select an option from the drop down menu.

Align Left will align the left side of the objects with the left edge of the left most selected object.

Align Centre will align the centre of the selected objects with the vertical centre of the selected object that is in the middle.

Align Right aligns the right side of the objects with the right edge of the right most selected object.

Align Top aligns the top side of the selected objects with the top edge of the top most selected object.

Align Middle aligns the selected objects in the horizontal middle of the selected object that is in the middle.

Align Bottom aligns the bottom side of the selected objects with the bottom edge of the bottom most selected object.

Distribute Objects

You can automatically distribute multiple objects evenly across your page. To do this, first select all the objects you want to distribute. Hold down the control key on your keyboard while you click the images you want to distribute.

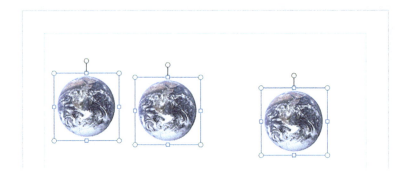

Click the 'picture tools' format ribbon and select 'arrange'. Click 'align'.

From the drop-down menu, select 'distribute horizontally' or 'distribute vertically'.

Distribute Horizontally will move the selected objects an equal distance apart horizontally across your selection.

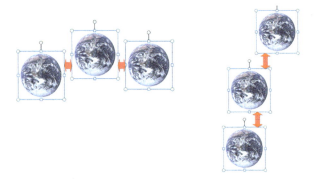

Distribute Vertically will move the selected objects an equal distance apart vertically across your selection.

Group Objects

You can group multiple objects into one object so they stay together if you move them. This is useful if you have created a graphic made up of multiple shapes and objects so you can resize and move without having to adjust each shape.

To do this, first select all the objects you want to group. Hold down the control key on your keyboard while you click the images.

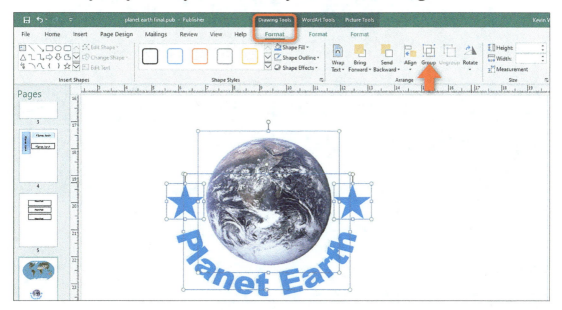

Select the 'drawing tools', or the 'picture tools' format ribbon then click 'group'.

You'll now be able to move the graphic as a single object.

To ungroup, select the object, then from the 'drawing tools' or the 'picture tools' format ribbon, select 'ungroup'.

Arranging Object Layers

Publications are constructed using transparent layers. Every time you add an object, text box, image, or shape you're adding it as a new layer on top. So a design like this:

Will have layers like this:

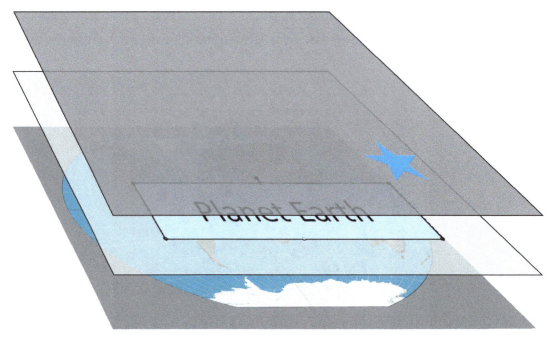

You can see the map is on the bottom layer, the text box is on top of the map, and the star is on top of the text box.

Now, if we wanted the star behind the text box we could change the layer arrangement. Select the star.

From the 'drawing tools' format ribbon, click 'send backward'.

Now you'll see the layer order change. The star will move behind the text box.

So you'll end up with something like this...

Page Parts

Publisher has some pre-designed building blocks to help you design your page. You can quickly add titles or sidebars to your page, as well as pre-formatted stories and quotes.

To add a page part, select the 'insert' ribbon, then click 'page parts'. Select a template from the drop down menu.

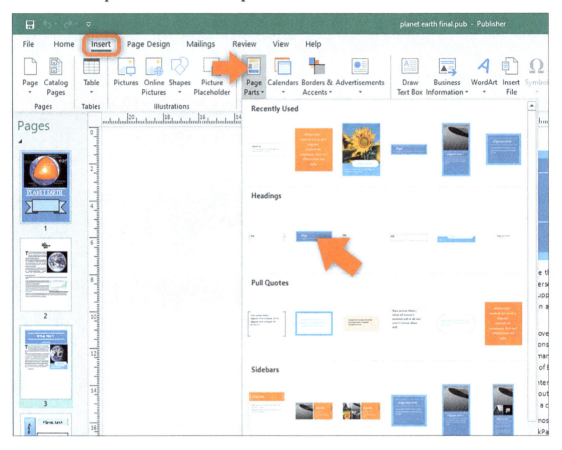

Click and drag the page part into position and resize it if necessary.

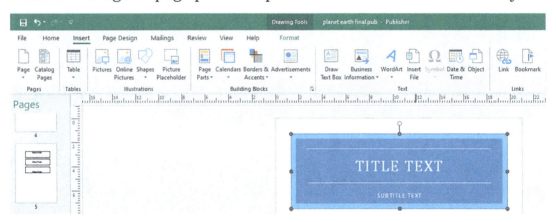

Type in your text in the place holders.

If there is an image, right click on the image then go down to 'change picture' and select 'change picture' from the slideout.

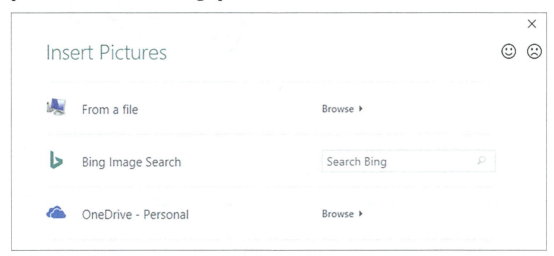

Select where you want to insert your picture from, then select your picture.

Chapter 5: Adding Graphics

If you want to change the colors. Click on the page part, then select the 'drawing tools' format ribbon.

From here you can use the shape fill to change the fill color, shape outline to change the border colors, and shape effects to add shadows or reflections to the page part.

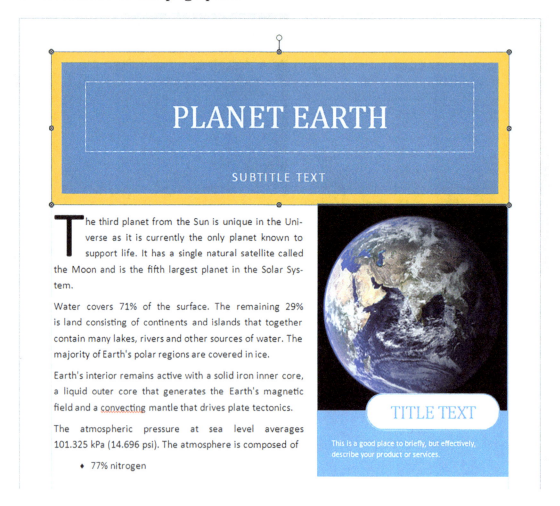

You can also use the shape style presets on this ribbon tab.

Select one and try it.

Borders & Accents

You can add borders to your page, image or text box. You can also add accents which are small decorations that can be used to emphasise other objects.

To add an accent, select your insert ribbon then click 'borders and accents'.

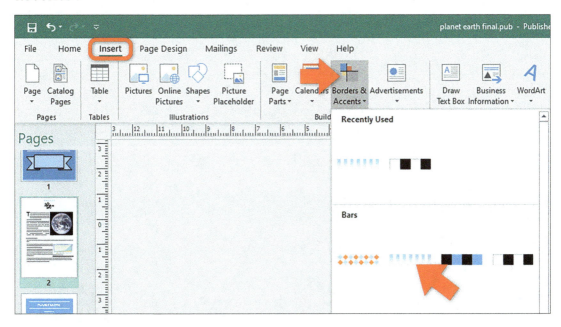

Resize and move the accent into position

Calendars

To add a calendar, select your insert ribbon then click 'calendars'. Select a template from the drop down menu.

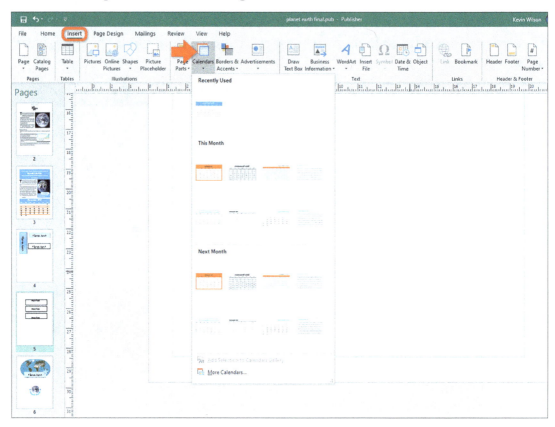

Resize and move your calendar into position.

If you need to add a calendar with a specific month, select 'more calendars' from the calendar drop down menu.

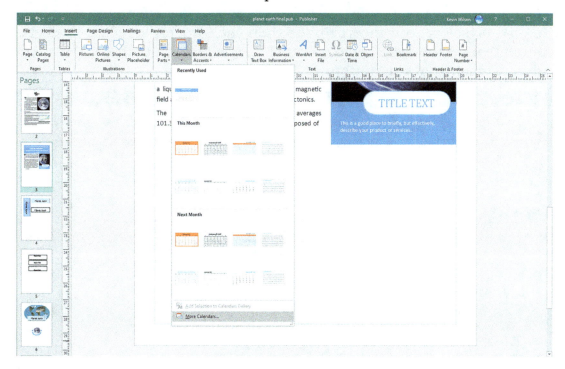

Select a template, then enter the month and year into the box on the right hand side. Click 'insert' when you're done.

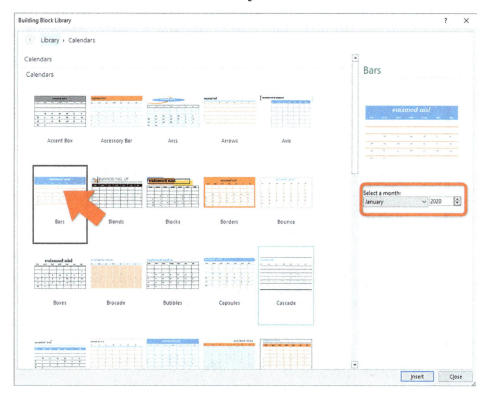

Advertisements

You can quickly create ads, attention grabbers, free offers and coupons. To do this, select your insert ribbon then click 'advertisements'. Select a template from the drop down menu. To see all ad templates, click 'more advertisements' at the bottom.

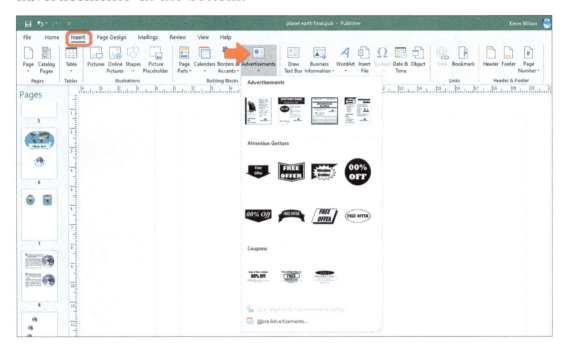

Resize and move the ad into place on your page.

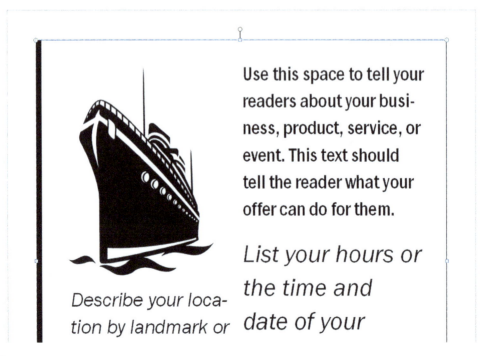

Type your information into the text boxes.

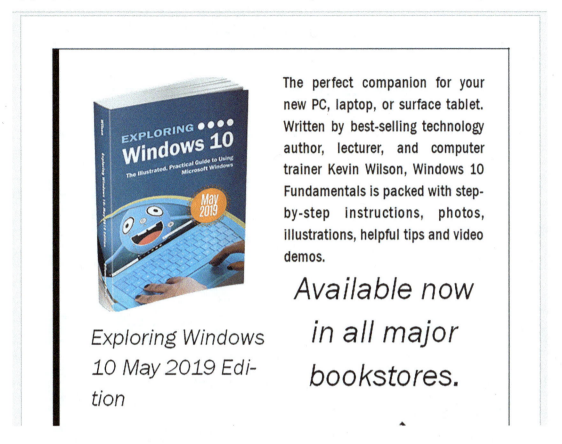

To change any images, right click on the image and click 'change image' then select 'change image' from the slideout.

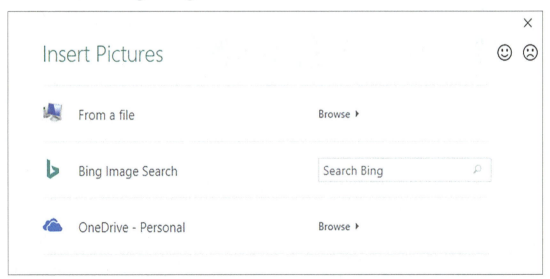

Select where you want to insert your picture from, then select your picture.

WordArt

WordArt is useful for creating headings and eye catching text. To add WordArt, click the 'insert' ribbon then select 'WordArt'. Select a style from the drop down menu.

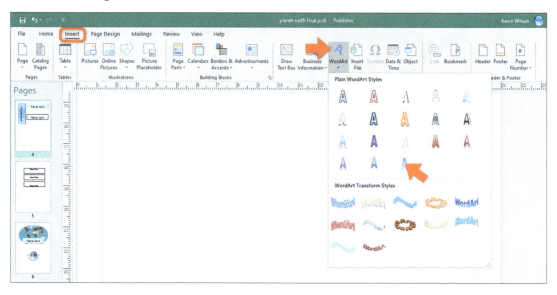

Select your font and size then enter your WordArt text.

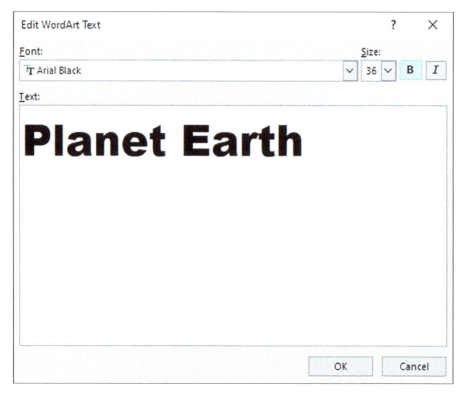

Click 'ok'.

From the WordArt Tools Format ribbon, you can change the style of the text using the presets.

Add a shadow or reflection effect using 'shape effects'.

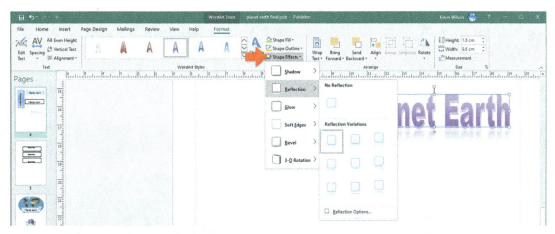

You can edit the color using 'fill color'.

Change the border of the text using 'shape outline'.

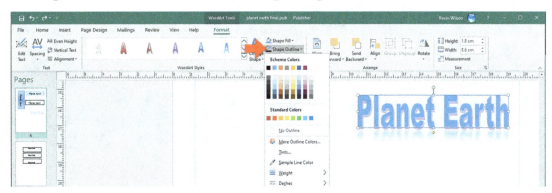

You can also change the shape of the text. To do this, click 'change shape'. Select a shape from the drop down menu.

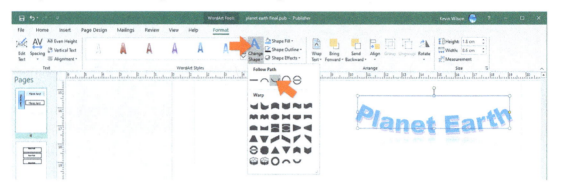

To adjust the shape, click and drag the small yellow handle on the WordArt.

Use the resize handles to resize your WordArt, use the rotate handle to rotate your WordArt.

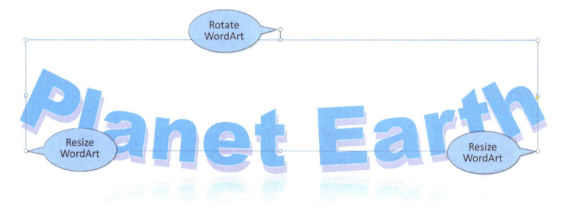

Images Types

There are generally two types of images: bitmap images and vector images.

Bitmap Images

Also known as raster images, uses thousands of pixels in varying colors and intensities to represent an image. Each pixel has a value, which specifies its color and location.

When you work with bitmap images, you are working with pixels, rather than shapes. This allows for gradations of color and creates a continuous tone appearance.

In the example above, because bitmap images contain a fixed number of pixels, they can lose detail or appear jagged edged when they are rescaled on the screen or printed at a higher resolution than they were created for.

You can see above, in the yellow circle, what happens to the image as the size increases - you start to see the pixels.

Vector Images

A vector graphic, on the other hand, is made up of polygons defined by mathematical formulas in 2D or 3D space.

Because of this, you can move, resize or change the color of the graphic without losing image quality.

This type of graphic is the best choice when you want a logo or bold graphic.

Image Resolution

Understanding how pixel data is measured and displayed, will help you make decisions about your images both when scanning and working with the images in Publisher.

The number of pixels in an image determines the quality and detail of that image.

Image resolution controls how much space these pixels are spread over when printed or displayed on screen. A high resolution image contains more and smaller pixels than an image with a low resolution. This means that a 1 x 1 inch image at 72 dpi would have 5184 pixels (72x72), whereas the same image at 300 dpi would have 90,000 pixels (300x300).

72 dpi

300 dpi

A higher resolution image produces more detail. However, increasing the resolution of an image only spreads the original pixel information over a larger number of pixels and will not improve image quality.

Most new monitors have a resolution of 96 dpi. No matter how high the resolution may be, we cannot see more than 96 pixels/inch in the displayed picture on a computer.

Printers vary widely, however your image should always be at least 300dpi if it is to be printed clearly.

Note PPI describes the resolution in pixels of a digital image whereas DPI describes the amount of ink dots on a printed image

Chapter 5: Adding Graphics

In Publisher, you can reduce the resolution of your pictures by compressing them. To do this, select the image. From the format ribbon click 'compress'.

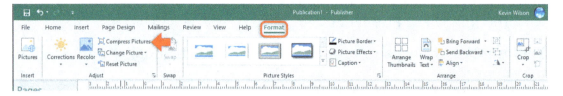

In the dialog box, under 'target output', select the print destination for your images:

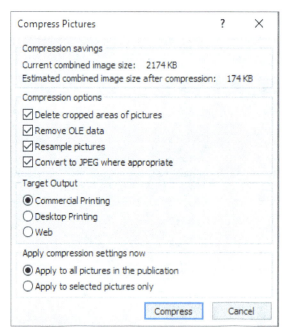

In the 'target output' section:

Click **commercial printing** to compress the pictures to 300 pixels per inch (ppi). Use this feature if you plan on sending the publication to a commercial printer.

Click **desktop printing** to compress the pictures to 220 ppi. Use this option if you intend on printing our your publication using a domestic or office inkjet/laser printer.

Click **web** to compress the pictures to 96 ppi. Use this option if you intend on publishing your work for viewing on the web.

Under 'apply compression settings now', choose whether you want to compress all pictures in the publication, or just the pictures that you selected, and then click 'compress'.

Common Image Formats

There are many different kinds of digital image file formats, each with their own capabilities and restrictions, here is a brief summary of the most common ones.

EPS "Encapsulated PostScript file" - used by programs such as PageMaker and Illustrator.

GIF A lossless image compression format, short for "Graphic Interchange Format" and is popular web icons, logos and buttons, but is limited to 8-bit (256 colors).

JPEG A lossy image compression format short for "Joint Photographic Experts Group" and is a popular format for saving photographs for use on the web or in printing.

PNG An image format using a lossless compression supporting 24-bit images (16.7 million colors) with transparency. This format is usually used on websites.

TIFF "Tagged Image File Format". These files tend to be either uncompressed or compressed using a lossless compression format and are commonly used in the printing and publishing industry.

WMF or Windows Meta File is a vector graphic format developed by Microsoft.

EMF or Enhanced Windows Metafile is an improved version of the Windows Metafile Format.

BMP is a raster image format developed by Microsoft. BMPs are usually are uncompressed and are large in file size.

RAW images are unprocessed files created by a camera or scanner, and usually have the image extension: raw, .cr2, .nef, .orf, or .sr2. Publisher wont read RAW files so you'll need to convert them first.

PSD file is an image file created by Adobe Photoshop. Publisher wont read PSD files so you'll need to convert them first.

Here is a full list according to Microsoft: Windows Bitmap (**BMP**), Tagged Image File Format (**TIFF** or **TIF**), Graphics Interchange Format (**GIF**), Encapsulated PostScript (**EPS**), Joint Photographics Expert Group (**JPEG** or **JPG**), Macintosh Picture (**PICT** or **PCT**), Compressed Macintosh PICT (**PC2**), Compressed Windows Metafile (**WM2**), Compressed Windows Enhanced Metafile (**EM2**), Kodak Photo CD (**PCD**), PC Paintbrush (**PCX**), Portable Network Graphics (**PNG**), CorelDraw (**CDR**), Computer Graphics Metafile (**CGM**), Windows Enhanced Metafile (**EMF**), FPX Format (**FPX**), Windows Metafile (**WMF**), WordPerfect Graphics (**WPG**), Picture It! Format (**MIX**).

Exercises

1. Open a new publication

2. Browse the internet, download an image and insert it into your publication

3. Resize the image to an appropriate size

4. Move the image into position

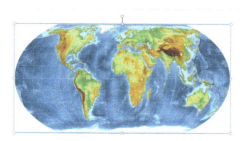

5. Change the color scheme of the image

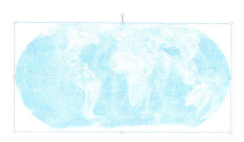

6. Add a word art image and place it at the top of the document as a heading.

7. Change the shape and fill color of the word art

8. Add a border and a shadow effect to the word art

9. You're working as a designer and a client comes to you. He owns a coffee shop and wants a flyer to promote his "grand opening" event. Create a flyer using the skills you learning in this chapter. Here's an example...

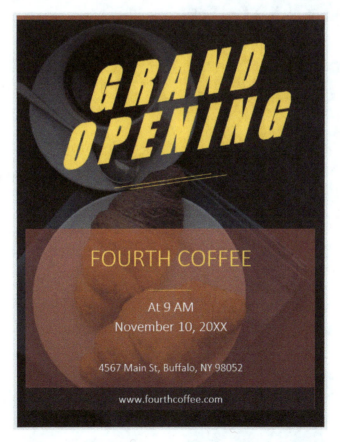

You'll need to add the name of the coffee shop, address, website and so on.

6

Mail Merge

In this section we'll take a look at creating a mail merge to create addressed envelopes and invites using Publisher.

We'll cover

- Mail Merge Templates
- Connecting a Data Source
- Inserting Merge Fields
- Mail Merge Envelopes
- Mail Merge an Invitation
- Printing Merged Publications

For this section you'll need the files from

elluminetpress.com/ms-pub

Scroll down to the files section and download the files.

Mail Merge Envelopes

If you have a lot of recipients, creating an envelope for each of them can be time consuming. This is where mail merge comes in handy.

First, you'll need to open an envelope template or create one. On the start up screen click 'new'. Scroll down and select 'built in', then click 'envelopes'.

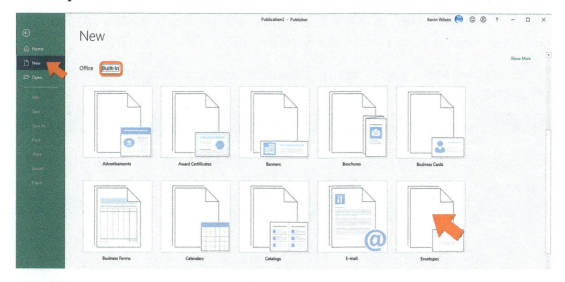

Scroll down to 'blank sizes' and select the size of envelope you're going to use. Click 'create'.

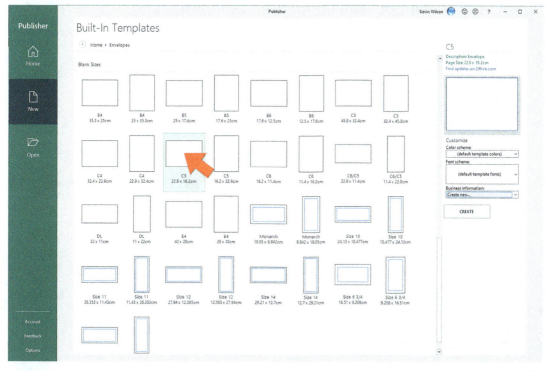

Chapter 6: Mail Merge

Next you'll need a data source. This is usually a list of names and addresses. A good place to keep names and addresses is in an excel spreadsheet. Also if you have added addresses to your Outlook 2019 contact list, you can import them from that.

I have a client list stored in an excel spreadsheet, so in this example, I will use that option. The procedure is the same if you use your Outlook contacts.

I have included some test data in a spreadsheet called Mail Merge Test Data.xlsx in the downloads section for you to practice with.

To select a data source, go to your mailings ribbon and click 'select recipients'.

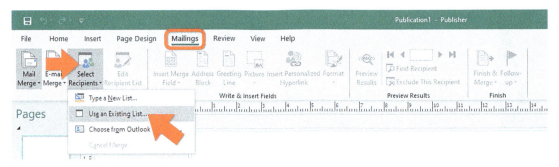

From the drop down menu, click 'use an existing list...'.

In the dialog box that appears, find your data source. I'm going to select my excel spreadsheet. Mail Merge Test Data.xlsx

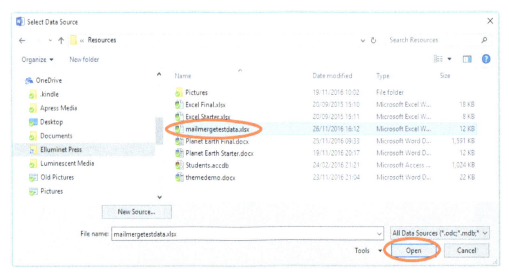

Click 'open'.

Click 'ok' on the next two dialog boxes.

Now to create your envelopes. From your mailings ribbon, click 'address block' to add the addresses from your contacts data source (Mail Merge Test Data.xlsx).

Resize your address block...

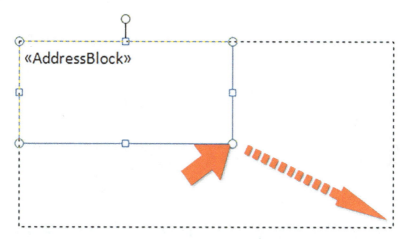

To preview your envelopes, from the mailings ribbon click 'preview results'. You can flip through the envelopes using the next/previous record icons.

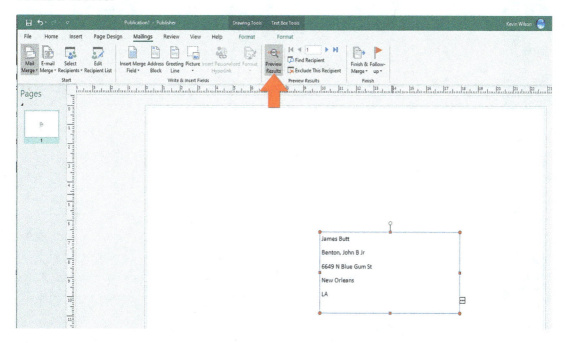

Chapter 6: Mail Merge

To finish off, from your mailings ribbon click 'finish & merge'. From the drop down menu, click 'print documents' to send the whole lot to the printer, make sure you have your envelopes already loaded into your printer's paper tray.

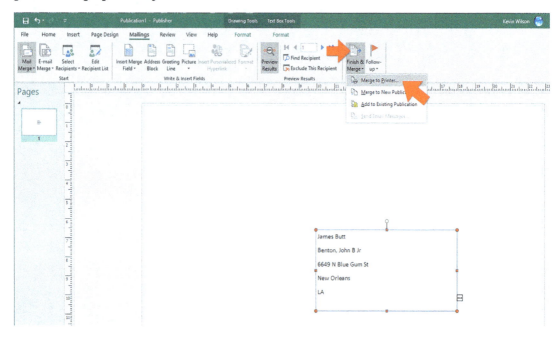

You can also click 'edit individual documents' and Word will generate a document with all your envelopes ready to print. This is useful if you want to make some changes or only print certain addresses.

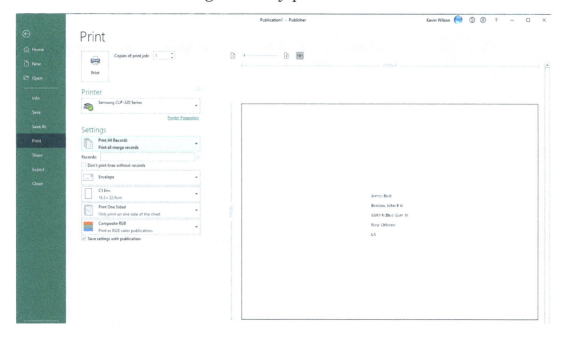

Select 'print all records' from the popup dialog box.

Mail Merge an Invitation

Now that we have our envelopes printed, we need to create our party invitation.

First open a template. On publisher's start screen, click 'new'. In the search field type in the publication template you want, in this example I'm creating a party invitation, so I'd type in 'party invitation'.

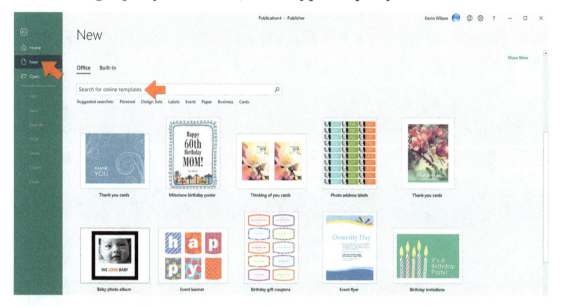

Double click the template you want.

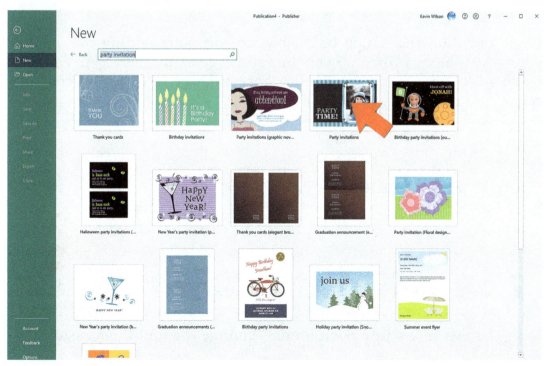

Chapter 6: Mail Merge

Next you need to add your data source. To connect your data source, select your mailings ribbon and click 'select recipients'. From the drop down menu, select 'use an existing list'.

Then select your data file. For this example, I'm using Mail Merge Test Data.xlsx.

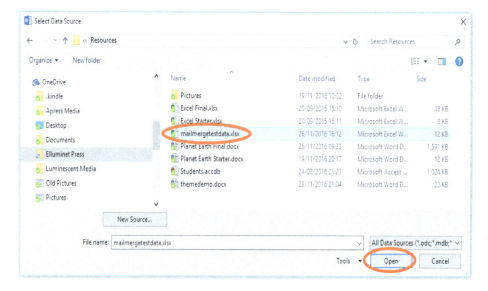

Click 'open' on the dialog box. Now we can start adding our names. From the mailings ribbon, click 'insert merge field', then from the drop down select 'first_name', then click 'insert merge field' and select 'last_name'.

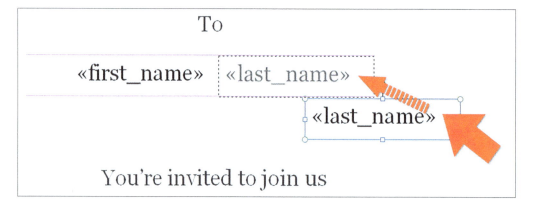

Drag the text boxes into position and change the font if necessary.

Once you have added all the fields, from the mailings ribbon click 'preview results'. You'll get something like this (a personalised invitation for each name):

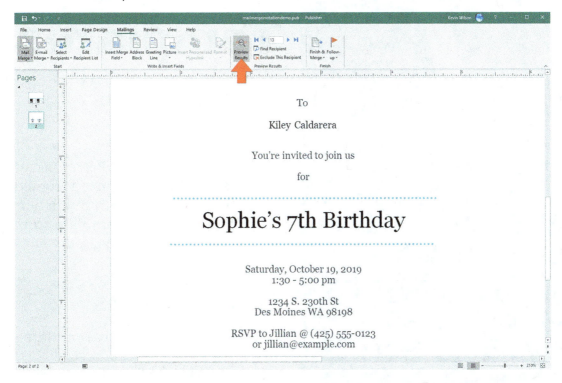

To finish off, from the mailings ribbon, click 'finish & merge'

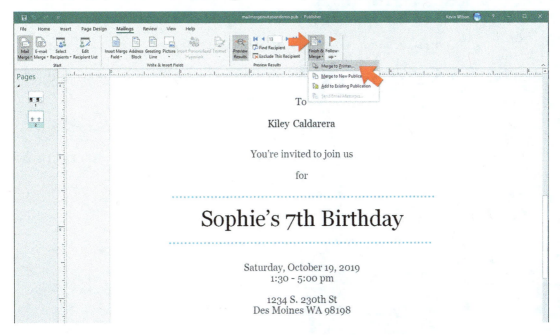

To send all letters to the printer click, 'print documents'.

7

Using Templates

In this section, we'll take a look at the many different pre-designed templates that come with publisher, as well as creating a template from scratch.

We'll cover

- Finding a Template
- Making Your Own Template
- Saving Templates

Check out the video resources. Open your browser and navigate to:

`elluminetpress.com/pub-man`

For this section you'll need the files from

`elluminetpress.com/ms-pub`

Scroll down to the files section and download the files.

Finding a Template

When you start Publisher, you will see a screen containing thumbnails of different templates that are available. To find templates, click 'new' on the left hand side.

The best way to find templates is to search for them.

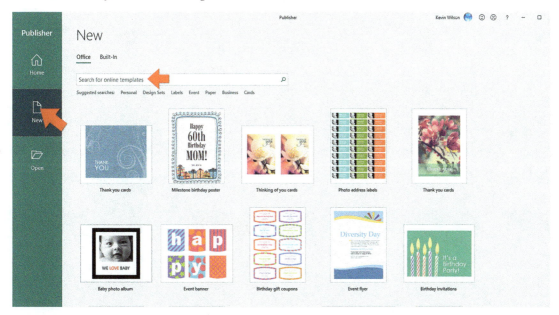

Why not try making a greeting card for someone you know?

Open Publisher, click 'new' on the left hand side and type...

```
greeting card
```

...into the search field.

Select a template to use from the search results. How about a nice Christmas card?

Double click the template thumbnail.

You can change the text or photo

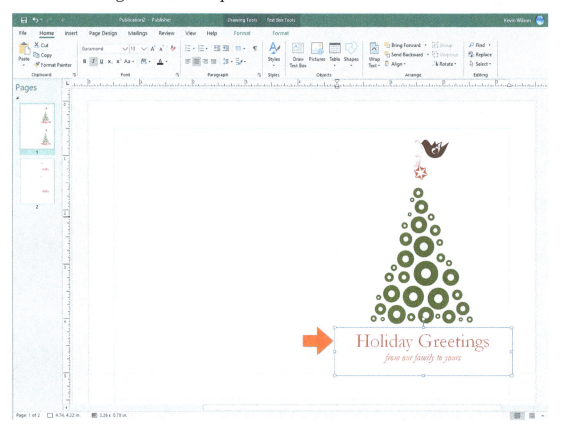

Just click on the text and enter your own.

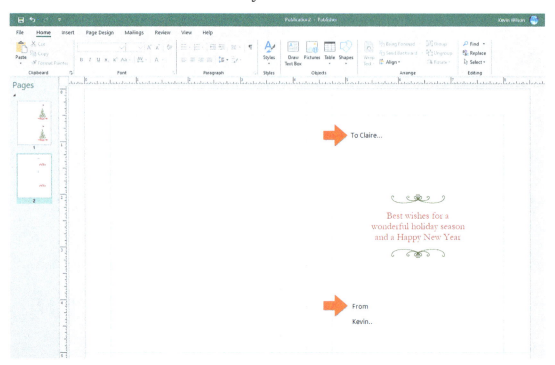

Making Your Own Template

If you have created your own style, eg heading sizes, fonts and layouts, you can save this as a template, so you can create new documents in the same style.

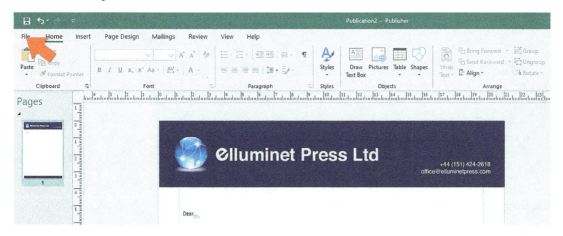

To save your publication as a template, select 'file' on the top left. From the backstage menu, select 'save as'. Select your 'onedrive' folder.

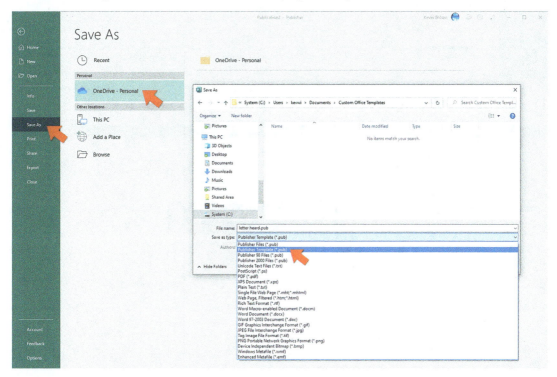

From the popup 'save as' dialog box, go down to 'save as type'. Change this to 'publisher template'

Click 'save'.

Chapter 7: Using Templates

To open a new file using the template, from the publisher start screen, click 'new'.

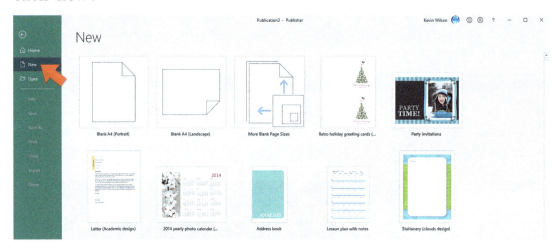

Scroll down and select 'personal'.

Double click your template. Now you can type in your text.

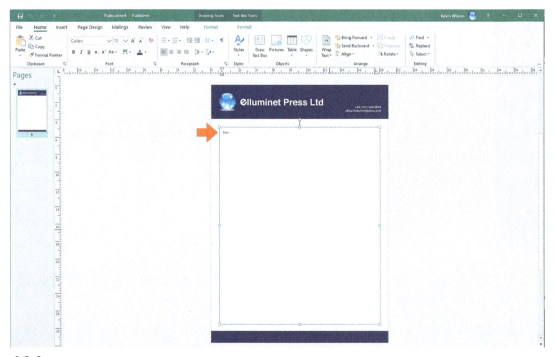

Save as a new publication. To do this, click 'file' on the top left of the screen.

Click 'save as'.

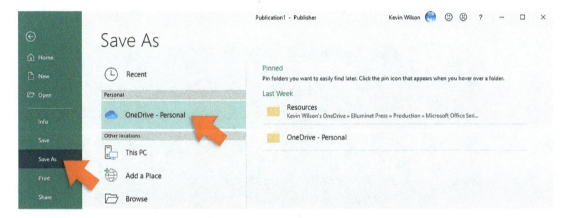

Select a folder to save your document in, and give the file a meaningful name.

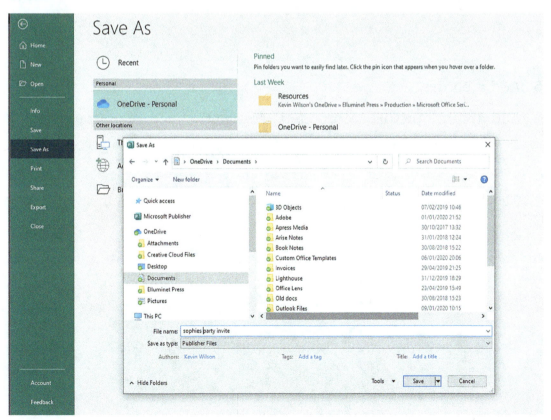

Exercises

1. Start publisher and open a template. It's a friend's birthday and you want to create a personalised card for them. Choose a template to begin with.

2. Change the title

3. Change the picture

4. Change the text colour

5. Add a border

6. Add another picture, rotate and arrange the picture on the page.

7. Save the current publication as a template

8. Open a new blank publication using the template you just saved

9. Save the new publication as a publisher document

10. Use a template to create a newsletter for your family, business or school. Here's an example:

8

Managing Publications

In this section we'll look at saving your work, printing, page setup and page masters.

We'll cover

- Saving Documents
- Saving as a Different Format
- Opening Saved Documents
- Page Setup
- Creating Booklets
- Page Tiling

Check out the video resources. Open your browser and navigate to:

elluminetpress.com/pub-man

For this section you'll need the files from

elluminetpress.com/ms-pub

Scroll down to the publisher section and download the files.

Saving Documents

To save your work, click the small disk icon in the top left hand corner of the screen.

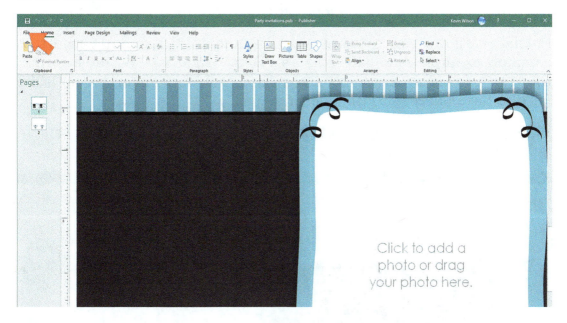

Click 'save as' on the left hand side. In the save as screen, you need to tell Publisher where you want to save the document. Double click on your OneDrive then from the dialog box, select where you want to save your publication (eg in 'documents').

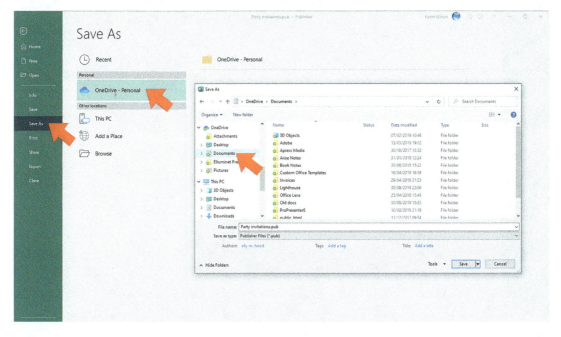

Give your file a name, in this case 'party invitations'. Click 'save'.

Saving as a Different Format

Sometimes you'll want to save a document in a different format. This can be useful if you are sending a document to someone that might not be using Windows or have Microsoft Office installed.

Publisher allows you to save your document in different formats. A common example is saving files as PDFs, which is a portable format that can be read on any type of computer, tablet or phone without the need to have Microsoft Publisher installed.

With your document open, click File on the top left of your screen. Select 'save as' from the list on the left hand side.

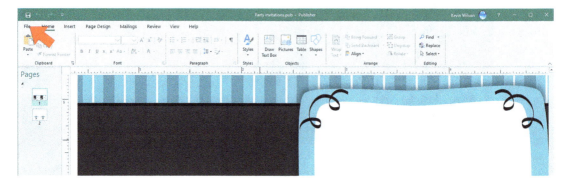

Double click 'OneDrive', select the folder you want to save the document into. Eg 'documents'.

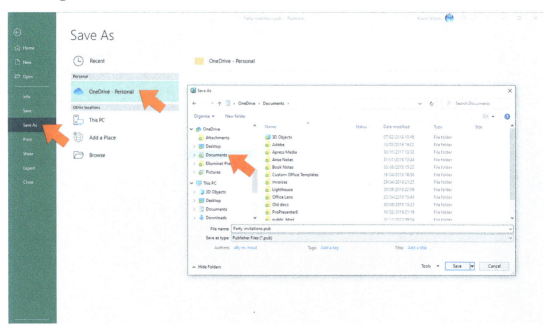

Give your file a name, in this case 'party invitations'.

Now to change the format, click the down arrow in the field below and from the list, click PDF.

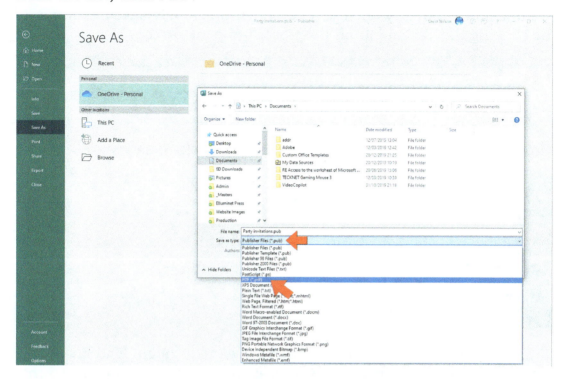

Select 'options' on the bottom left of the dialog box.

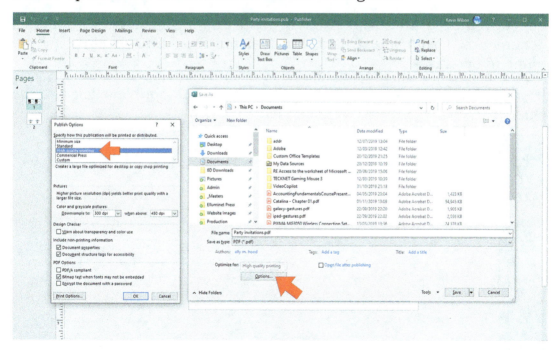

Select high quality printing, then click 'ok'. Click 'save' on the 'save as' dialog box.

Opening Saved Documents

If Publisher is already open you can open previously saved documents by clicking the 'file' menu on the top left of your screen.

From the green bar along the left hand side click 'open'.

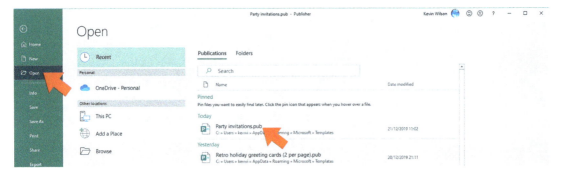

From the list, select the document you want to open. The document from the previous project was saved as 'party invitations.pub', so this is the one I am going to open here.

For convenience, Microsoft Publisher lists all your most recently opened documents.   Your latest files will be listed first. Double click the file name to open it.

If your document is saved on your OneDrive, double click on the OneDrive icon to browse the files. Select your file.

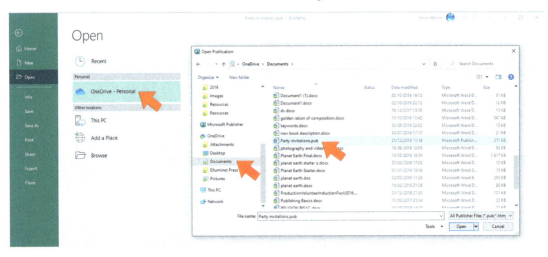

Click 'open'.

Page Setup

Page setup allows you to adjust margins, paper size, orientation (landscape/portrait) and general layout.

To adjust your page setup, go to your 'page design' tab and click the expand icon on the bottom right of the page setup section.

From the dialog box that appears, you can adjust the layout type meaning you can create a booklet layout, envelope, full page, etc

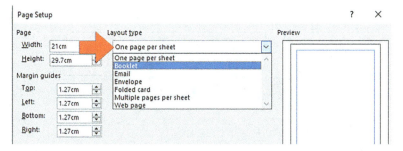

You can adjust the margins as shown below using the 'margin guides'.

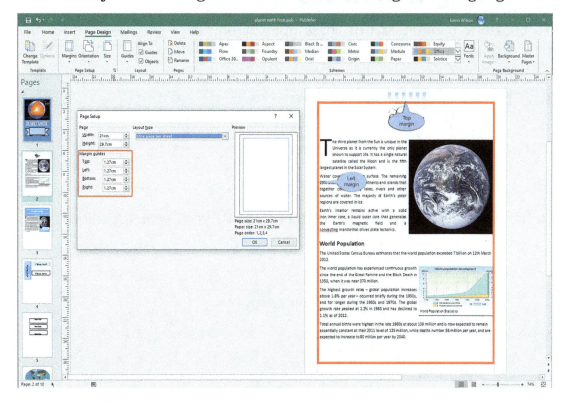

You can also adjust the page size.

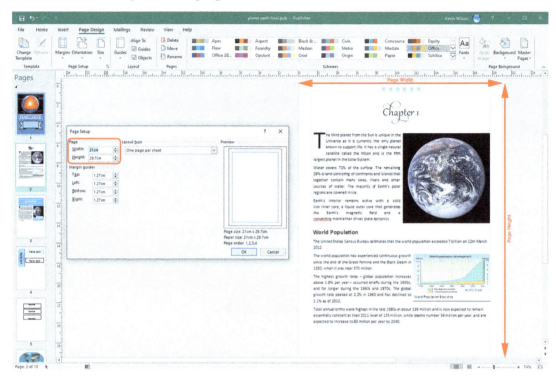

Creating Booklets

To create a booklet layout, first open a blank publication. From the page design ribbon tab, click the icon on the bottom right of the 'page setup' section.

In the 'page setup' dialog box, under 'layout type', select 'booklet'.

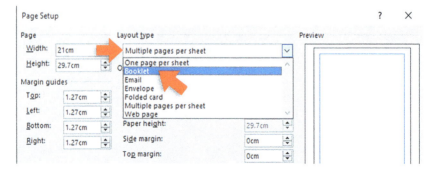

Once you click 'ok', Publisher will create a booklet layout for you. On the left hand side of your screen you'll see your pages in the navigation pane. Here, you have your front page, then the inside spread and the back page.

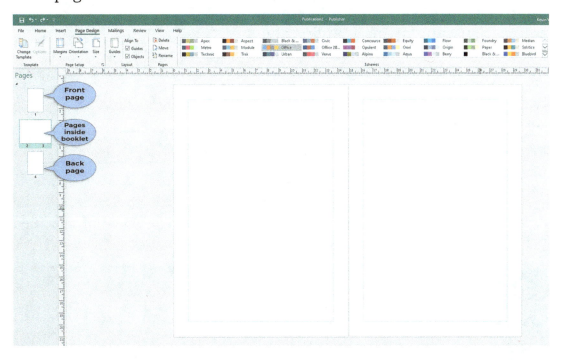

Now you can start to build your booklet. This is the best way to start. If you convert a publisher document to booklet form you may have problems with layout if publisher needs to resize pages.

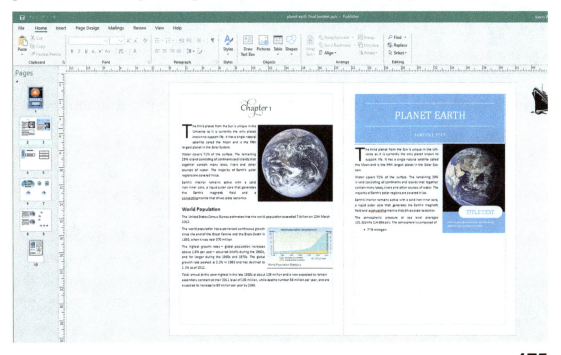

Tiling Pages

This is useful if your printer only prints A4 or A3 at its largest and you want to print a banner that is much bigger. You can do this by tiling the publication across multiple pages and then glueing the pages together.

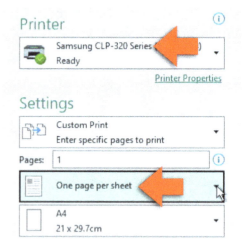

Select 'file' on the top left of the screen, then click on print.

From the printer settings, select your printer. Then from the page options select 'tiling'.

Select the page orientation and size. You'll see a preview of the tiled printout and the number of pages it will use. Click 'print'.

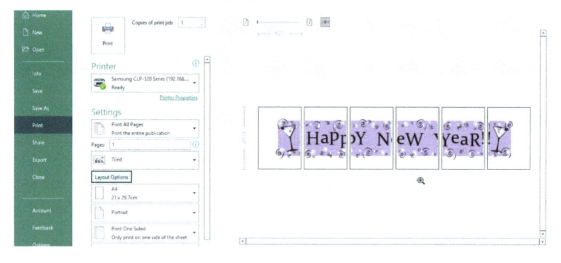

Once it is printed, you can stick the banner together using paper glue.

Once you've stuck the pages together, you can trim the banner accordingly.

Exercises

1. Create a new publication

2. Change the page size to 15.24cm x 22.86cm

3. Set the top, bottom and right margins to 2cm

4. Set the left margin to 3cm

9

Publishing your Work

Will you be printing? Publishing electronically? In this section, we'll take a look at printing, exporting and sharing your publications.

You can print your documents using your own printer or you can export your document as a PDF or share the document with someone over email.

We'll cover

- Design checks
- How to Publish your Work
- Printing Documents
- Print as Booklet
- Export as PDF
- Share a File
- Other Formats

Check out the video resources. Open your browser and navigate to:

elluminetpress.com/pub-print

Design Checker

The design checker is an automated tool that scans your publication for errors such as empty frames, overflow text in textboxes, objects left in the non-printing region and objects that are covered or not visible.

To start the design check, click on 'file'.

Select 'info' from the list on the left. Scroll down the page, then click on 'run design checker'.

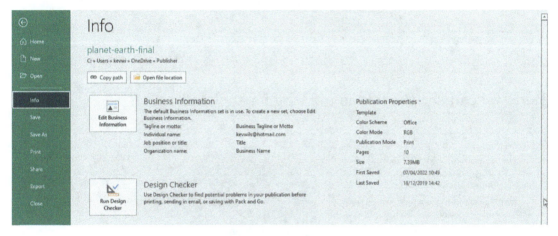

Publisher will run through your publication and highlight any potential errors it finds. These will be listed in the design check sidebar on the right hand side of the screen.

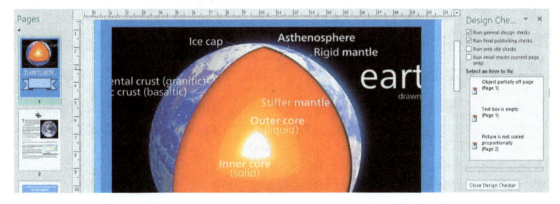

Make sure you select 'run general design checks' and 'run final publishing checks'. You only need to enable 'run website checks' and 'run email checks' if you intend on publishing your work online as a webpage.

Here, we can see publisher has picked up a few potential issues. In this particular example, publisher has highlighted a textbox where the text is cut off. Click on the issue to see the error.

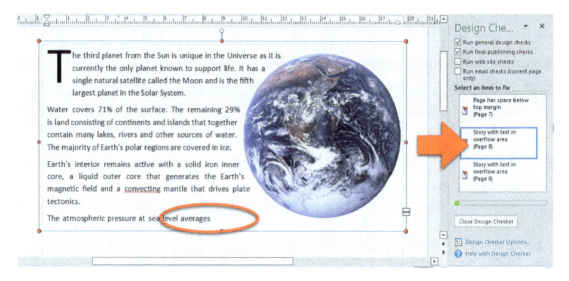

Here, we can see the text is too long for the textbox.

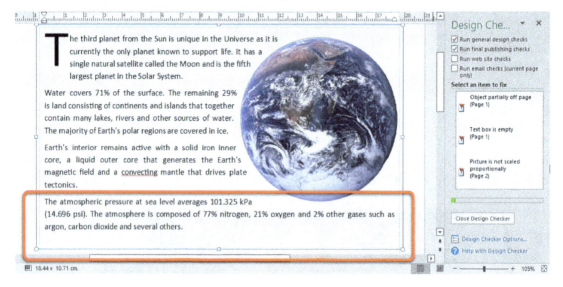

To correct this, you can either increase the size of the textbox, or decrease the size of the font if there is no space to make the textbox bigger. In this example, I've lengthened the textbox so the cut off text is visible. There will be various other issues, and you can go through them but some of them you can ignore.

To change the design check options, click on 'design check options' at the bottom of the sidebar on the right hand side. In the dialog box under the 'checks' tab, you can select or deselect the checks you want to perform.

Spell Check

To check the spelling in your publication, click on the 'review' ribbon tab.

Select 'spelling'. The spell check will check the spelling in the currently selected text box. If you have multiple text boxes throughout your publications, you'll receive a prompt asking you to check the rest of your publication. Click 'yes'.

The spell check will highlight any words it thinks are misspelled. Here, the spell check has highlighted the word 'coverd'. Select the correct spelling in the suggestions, then click 'change'.

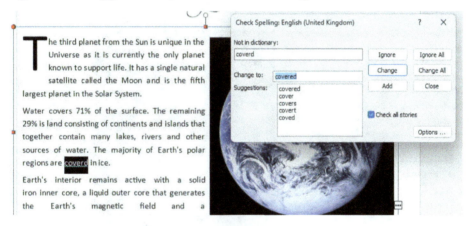

Sometimes the spell check will highlight words it doesn't recognise - usually proper nouns such as a person's name or place name. To add the word to the dictionary, click add'.

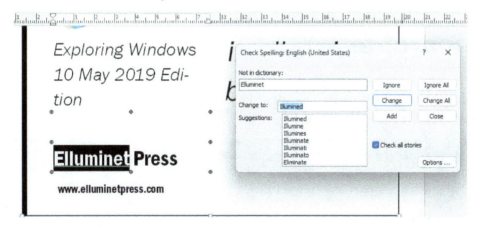

Thesaurus

A thesaurus is useful for finding alternative words to make your writing sound better. To do this, highlight the word you want to find an alternative for. Click on 'thesaurus' in the 'review ribbon' tab.

In the panel that opens up on the right hand side, scroll down the synonyms for a suitable alternative word. In this example, I've selected the word 'interior'. An alternative that would still make sense in the sentence would be 'centre'. Right click on the word in the thesaurus, select 'insert' from the menu.

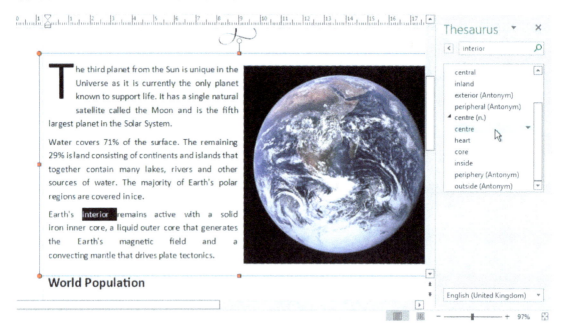

Researcher

The researcher is useful for getting additional information about a word in your publication. To find information, click on 'research' in the 'review ribbon' tab.

A panel will open up on the right hand side. Hold down the 'alt' key on your keyboard, then click on the word you want to research. In this example, I'm going to research the word 'sun'.

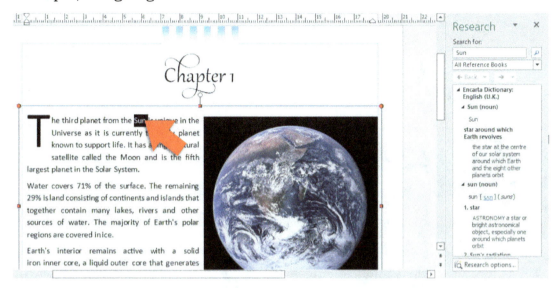

In the panel on the right hand side, you'll see a list of definitions and information

Translate

You can translate a word or selected text into another language. Keep in mind that the translation isn't perfect, so the translated text might not read correctly to a native speaker of the language.

To do this, highlight the word or text you want to translate. Click on 'translate' in the 'review ribbon' tab.

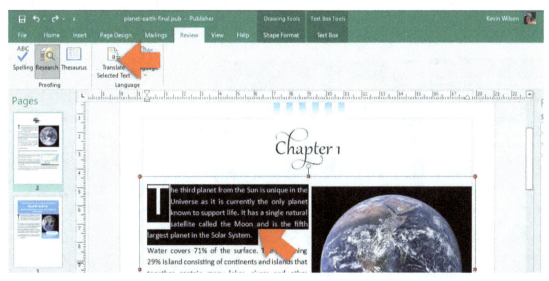

In the panel on the right hand side, select the language you want to translate the text into. In this example, I'm going to translate the text into Spanish.

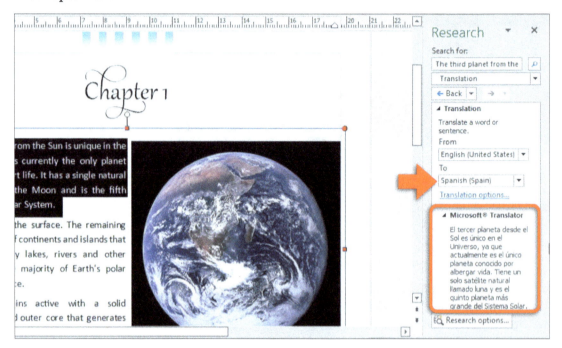

You'll see the translation appear underneath the selections. Click 'insert'. If you want to insert the translation in place of the selected text, click 'insert', otherwise click 'copy' to copy the translation to the clipboard.

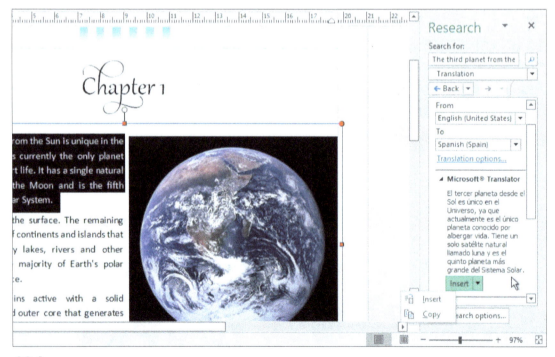

Printing Documents

To print a document, click 'file' on the top left of your screen.

Select 'print' from the green bar along the left of the screen.

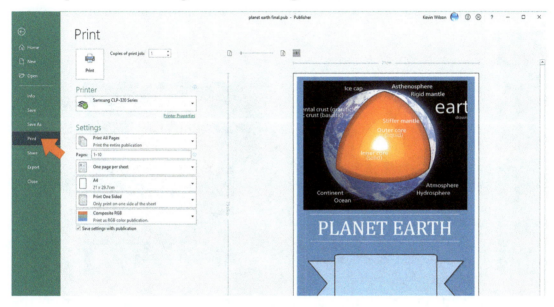

You can select options such as number of copies, print individual pages or print all pages.

You can print the page on one sheet of paper or scale it up to multiple sheets. Or you can print multiple pages on a single sheet. You can also print the pages into a booklet. To change this setting click the 'one page per sheet' drop down menu.

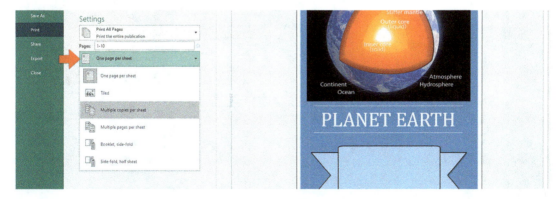

Once you have set all your options, click the print button at the top.

Print as Booklet

Open your publication. To print as a booklet, select 'file' on the top left of the screen,

Select 'print' from the green bar along the left hand side of the screen.

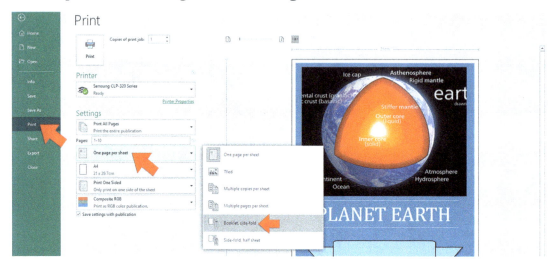

From the 'settings' section, go down to 'one page per sheet'. From the popup menu, select 'booklet side fold'.

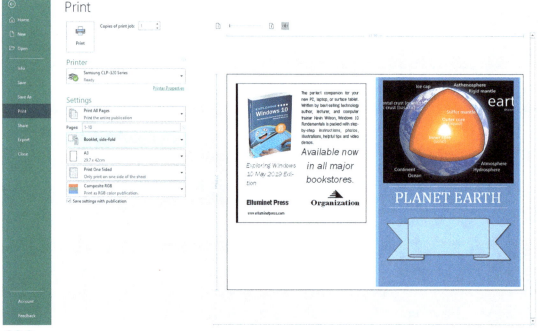

Most modern printers support duplex printing (ie printing on both sides of the paper). With some desktop printers, choosing duplex means that the printer prints all of the copies of the first side of a page, then pauses and asks you to flip the sheets that it just printed and return them to the printer. Then it prints all of the copies of the second side.

To print on both sides, click the drop down box that says 'print one sided'

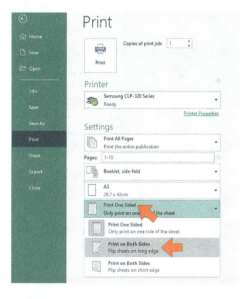

Click 'print' at the top of the screen.

If printing on both sides of the page, once the printer has printed the first side, turn the whole stack of printed sheets over and put them back into the paper tray.

Export as PDF

Click File on the top left of your screen.

Select 'export' from the list on the left hand side. Select 'create PDF/XPS Document', then click the 'create PDF/XPS' button.

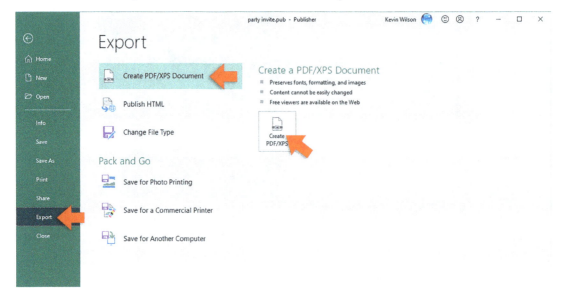

Select where you want to save the PDF file, give it a meaningful name, then click 'options' at the bottom of the window.

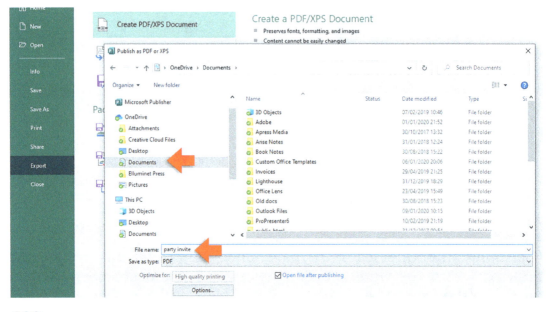

Select your publishing options depending on where you are publishing your document to. For example, if you are sending your publication to a commercial printer, then select 'commercial press'

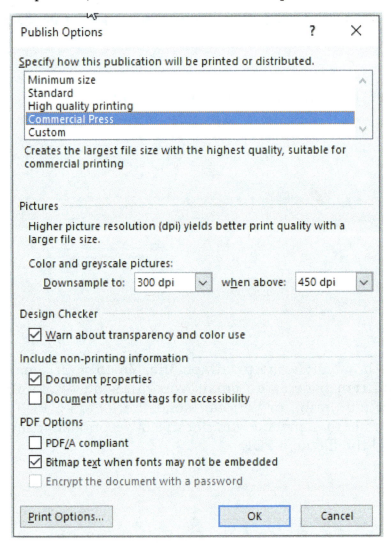

Adjust the PDF options according to the printing press you're using. If not then you can leave them as they are.

Click 'ok'.

Click 'publish' in the save dialog box.

Share a File

Click File on the top left of your screen.

Select 'share' from the list on the left hand side.

Now select how you want to attach the file to your email. You can send the current page as an email, you can send your publication as a publisher file (.pub), or you can send the file as a PDF. If you are sending the file to someone who doesn't have publisher installed, you should send the file as a PDF.

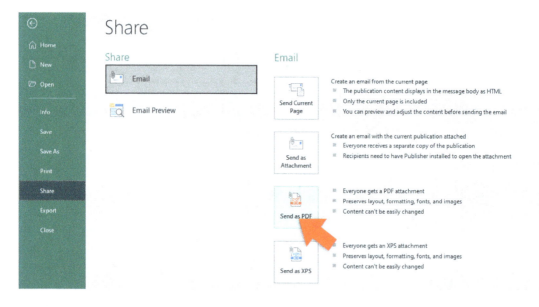

In this example I'm going to send as PDF. So I'd click 'send as PDF'.

Once the email opens up, you'll see the file attached to the email. Add the email address of the person you're sending the file to, add a subject and a message.

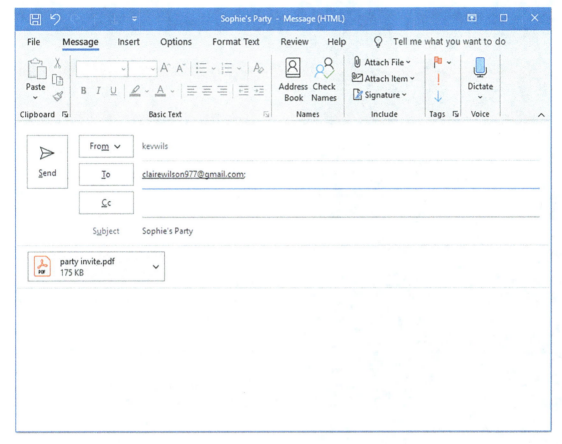

Click 'send' when you're done.

Resources

To help you understand the procedures and concepts explored in this book, we have developed some video resources and app demos for you to use, as you work through the book.

To find the resources, open your web browser and navigate to the following website

`elluminetpress.com/ms-pub`

At the beginning of each chapter, you'll find a website that contains the resources for that chapter.

File Resources

To save the files into your OneDrive documents folder, right click on the icons above and select 'save target as' (or 'save link as', on some browsers). In the dialog box that appears, select 'OneDrive', click the 'Documents' folder, then click 'save'.

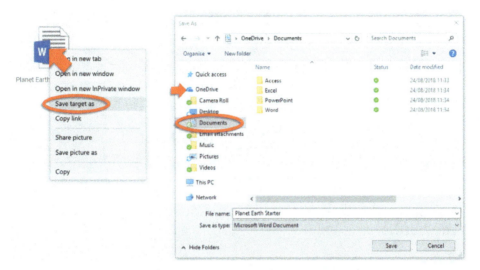

The sample images are stored in a compressed zip file. To download the zip file, right click on the zip icon on the page above, 'Sample Images. zip. Select 'save target as' (or 'save link as', on some browsers) and save it into 'pictures' on your OneDrive folder.

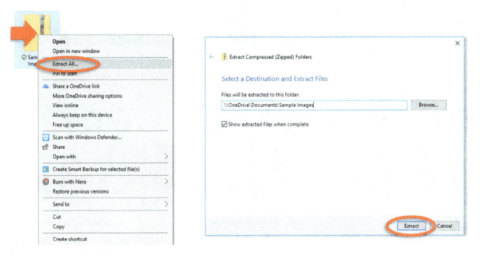

Once you have downloaded the zip file, go to your 'pictures' folder in your OneDrive, right click on the zip file, and select 'extract all' from the menu. From the dialog box that appears click 'extract'. This will create a new folder in your pictures called 'sample images'. You'll find the images used in the examples in the books.

Video Resources

The video resources are grouped into sections for each chapter in the book. Click the thumbnail link to open the section.

When you open the link to the video resources, you'll see a thumbnail list at the bottom.

Click on the thumbnail for the particular video you want to watch. Most videos are between 30 and 60 seconds outlining the procedure, others are a bit longer.

When the video is playing, hover your mouse over the video and you'll see some controls...

Let's take a look at the video controls. On the left hand side:

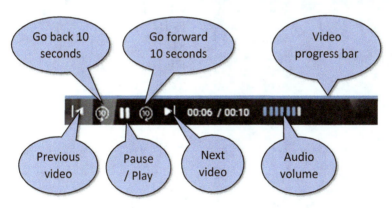

On the right hand side:

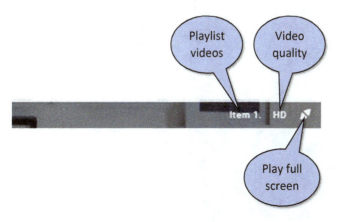

Index

Index

Index

SOMETHING
NOT COVERED?

We want to create the best possible resources to help you learn and get things done, so if we've missed anything out, then please get in touch using the links below and let us know. Thanks.

 office@elluminetpress.com

 elluminetpress.com/feedback

www.ingramcontent.com/pod-product-compliance
Lightning Source LLC
LaVergne TN
LVHW062316060326

832902LV00013B/2247